P9-CLL-557

GHOLDY MUHAMMAD

Cultivating Genius

AN EQUITY FRAMEWORK FOR CULTURALLY AND HISTORICALLY RESPONSIVE LITERACY

To Al Mujib (The Responsive).

I dedicate this book to my mothers:
Maria, Ajile, Evelyn, and Bernice.

And to my Baba.

Photos ©: cover and throughout: johnwoodcock/Getty Images; 24: Monkey Business Images/Shutterstock; 31: Accessible Archives Inc.®; 41: SDI Productions/iStockphoto; 46 top: Bongani Mnguni/City Press/Gallo Images/Getty Images; 46 bottom: AP Photo/Bill Hudson; 47: Courtesy of Oregon Historical Society; 48: kali9/iStockphoto; 53: Wilson Group Network, Inc.; 55: kali9/iStockphoto; 62: SDI Productions/iStockphoto; 66: Iakov Filimonov/Shutterstock; 71: Paul Popper/Popperfoto/Getty Images; 73: xavierarnau/iStockphoto; 83: Bettmann/Getty Images; 89: Monkey Business Images/Shutterstock; 106: wavebreakmedia/Shutterstock; 130: General Research Division, The New York Public Library; 131: Zurijeta/Shutterstock; 136: SpeedKingz/Shutterstock; 140: University of Detroit Mercy, Special Collections, Black Abolitionist Archive; 151: Library of Congress. All other photos by Josh Moïse for Scholastic Inc.

Excerpt from "Hidden Name and Complex Fate" from *Shadow and Act* by Ralph Ellison. Copyright © 1953, 1964 by Ralph Ellison. Reprinted by permission of the Ralph and Fanny Ellison Charitable Trust and Random House, Inc., a division of Penguin Random House LLC. All rights reserved.

Excerpt from *To Be a Slave* by Julius Lester. Copyright © 1968 by Julius Lester. Reprinted by permission of Penguin Young Readers Group, a division of Penguin Random House LLC. All rights reserved.

Excerpt from *Long Walk to Freedom: The Autobiography of Nelson Mandela* by Nelson Mandela. Copyright © 1994, 1995 by Nelson Rolihlahla Mandela. Reprinted by permission of Little, Brown and Company, a division of Hachette Book Group, Inc. All rights reserved.

Excerpt from the speech "What Is Your Life's Blueprint?" delivered by Dr. Martin Luther King Jr. to students at Barratt Junior High in Philadelphia on October 26, 1967. Copyright © 1967 by Dr. Martin Luther King Jr., renewed © 1991 by Coretta Scott King. Reprinted by arrangement with The Heirs to the Estate of Martin Luther King Jr., c/o Writers House as agent for the proprietor New York, NY. All rights reserved.

Excerpt from the speech "Where Do We Go From Here?" delivered by Dr. Martin Luther King Jr. at the Eleventh Annual SCLC Convention in Atlanta on August 16, 1967. Copyright © 1967 by Dr. Martin Luther King Jr., renewed © 1986 by Coretta Scott King. Reprinted by arrangement with The Heirs to the Estate of Martin Luther King Jr., c/o Writers House as agent for the proprietor New York, NY. All rights reserved.

Publisher: Lois Bridges
Editorial director: Sarah Longhi
Editor-in-Chief: Raymond Coutu
Development/production editor: Danny Miller
Senior editor: Shelley Griffin
Assistant editor: Molly Bradley
Editorial assistant: Sean Cavanagh
Cover designer: Tom Martinez
Interior designer: Maria Lilja

Scholastic is not responsible for the content of third-party websites and does not endorse any site or imply that the information on the site is error-free, correct, accurate, or reliable.

No part of this publication may be reproduced in whole or in part, or stored in a retrieval system, or transmitted in any form or by any means, electronic, mechanical, photocopying, recording, or otherwise, without written permission of the publisher. For information regarding permission, write to Scholastic Inc., 557 Broadway, New York, NY 10012.

Copyright © 2020 by Gholdy Muhammad.
All rights reserved. Published by Scholastic Inc.
Printed in the U.S.A.

ISBN-13: 978-1-338-59489-8

SCHOLASTIC and associated logos are trademarks and/or registered trademarks of Scholastic Inc.
Other company names, brand names, and product names are the property and/or trademarks of their respective owners. Scholastic does not endorse any product or business entity mentioned herein.

2 3 4 5 6 7 8 9 10   40   28 27 26 25 24 23 22 21 20

♻ Text pages printed on 10% PCW recycled paper.

Scholastic Inc., 557 Broadway, New York, NY 10012

Contents

Go to **scholastic.com/GeniusResources** to access professional resources for this book, including videos featuring Gholdy Muhammad.

Acknowledgments

Sisters—I would like to express gratitude to the beautiful and brilliant Black women in my life who have kept me, supported me, and lifted me.

Akilah Muhammad, my big sister. Thank you for always believing in me and for helping to raise me.

To my best friend, Yolanda Sealey-Ruiz. You are the epitome of sisterhood and friendship. You teach me more about faith with each growing day. With your joy and love, I know that all will be good in the world.

To sisters—Trudie, Quran, Sherell, Chels, Bettina, Terri, Nya, Ebony, Dr. Dillard, LaTavia, Ashtria, Angela, Alexis (Ali), Natina, Drina, Tiff, Ahkillah, Marcelle, Detra, Maima, Glenda, Francheska, Ruby, Elise, Safiyah, Maisha, Valerie, Elizabeth, and Dr. Smith.

A special acknowledgment to sisters and mentors Jennifer Boykins and Karen Proctor. You are models of greatness. Thank you for believing in this work from day one.

Brothers—Thank you Umar—for loving me and my mind.

Thanks to Abdullah, Salah, Abdur, Muhammad, Harlan, Cherrod, Lee Gonzalez, Darrell, Nafis, Diallo, Joe, Nickolaus, Marc, Pedro, and David.

And to Imams Nadim and Plemin. Shukraan.

Special gratitude to my mentor, Alfred Tatum. You designed a course while I was a doctoral student. In this class, I started studying 1800s Black literary societies, and it was this foundation from which this book emerged. You have taught me to use my pen in urgent and unapologetic ways, and for this I am deeply grateful.

Thank you, Lois Bridges, for loving this book so much! I can only hope others carry that same contentment.

Finally, writing this book was such an act of joy due to the work and collaboration with New York City educators. Thank you for your energy, criticality, and for all that you do for our children. Ubuntu.

Foreword by Bettina L. Love

To know Gholdy Muhammad is to know love. To see her teach is to witness what the great Dr. Asa Hillard called a Master Teacher. To hear her lecture, you quickly realize she is unmatched in her ability to articulate why literacy is important beyond the surface of learning how to read and write, as a necessary tool for justice, equity, and a world where the humanity and dignity of those pushed to the edges of society are front and center. She embodies this work, and I am forever grateful to know that she is among the amazing folx fighting for the lives of Black and Brown children to matter.

This book is simply brilliant. It is Gholdy's literacy love letter for helping teachers cultivate the genius of Black and Brown children. What she has written is a way to see literacy through a framework that does not run from our current political times and embraces both the diversity of learning and the diversity of our children, all while doing the work of connecting children to who they are. You must know who you are and why you are important to this world, and learn how to be you. And this is particularly true for our Black and Brown children—because this world will constantly tell you that you are not good enough based on the color of your skin.

Gholdy's four-layered Historically Responsive Literacy framework includes identity development, skill development, intellectual development, and criticality. This equity framework uses literacy to make our children whole. Black folx and folx of color in this country have always used language, guided by history, to resist, because we understand that our rights and our dignity are tightly knitted together to our history and language.

This book is written in the tradition of Ella Baker, Ida B. Wells, bell hooks, Gloria Anzaldúa, Angela Davis, and Cherríe Moraga. Those women knew that fighting for justice in solidarity with each other is a beautiful struggle, and that words must be the foundation. In education, we have allowed terms like "at risk," "disadvantaged," and "struggling reader" to define our children, never considering that those terms have a history, too. As Gholdy points out, this deficit language that frames Black and Brown children's educational experience is rooted in and guided by Whiteness. It is precisely for that reason that strategies like "racing to the top" and "leaving no child behind" always fail because we are not teaching to repair and make our children feel whole and loved through their own identities, skills, intellect, and criticality.

There are many paths to a liberating education. *Cultivating Genius* is one that is needed both before and after liberation. Gholdy's groundbreaking book provides urgent pedagogy for urgent times. Gholdy placed love at the center of her method for teaching students, and you will, in turn, love this book and its message that meaning-making of children's stories is the way to humanize ourselves, which must happen before we enter the classroom.

Gholdy has written the new blueprint for how we teach responsive literacy. The Black Literary Societies of the 1800s, of which she so eloquently writes, would be proud. She has picked up the legacy and is running toward freedom. We in education need to follow and run with her.

Bettina L. Love is an associate professor of educational theory and practice at the University of Georgia. She is the author of *We Want to Do More Than Survive: Abolitionist Teaching and the Pursuit of Educational Freedom*.

Restoring Equity and Excellence in Today's Classrooms

> I conceive our Literary Institutions to have the power of doing. It seems to me, then, that the main object is to accomplish an intellectual and moral reformation. And I know of but few better ways to effect this than by reading, by examining, by close comparisons and thorough investigations, by exercising the great faculty of thinking; for, if a man can be brought to think, he soon discovers that his highest enjoyment consists in the improvement of the mind; it is this that will give him rich ideas, and teach him, also, that his limbs were never made to wear the chains of servitude; he will see too that equal rights were intended to all. Then who would not wish to become inspired with the taste of reading, if it has the ability to create so happy a state of things as I have just described.
>
> —James Forten in an address delivered before the American Moral Reform Society, August 17, 1837

Throughout the 1800s, a central objective among Black people was to improve and elevate their lives through literary means. One of the ways in which they set out to counter the conditions they endured during a time of racism and oppression was through reading, writing, and engaging with literary texts. As part of a broader struggle to counter multiple attacks of oppression with violence, they used their minds and pens as weapons to battle injustice. Books and other forms of texts became ammunition to fuel their progress. They worked toward cultivating the minds and hearts within themselves and among others, which led them to being equipped to face and alter the nation's harshest realities. Literacy was no longer just a set of skills to possess, but the instruments used to define their lives and the tools to advocate for their rights. To this end, Black people developed literary societies or "literary institutions," which were essentially collaborative teaching and learning spaces to construct knowledge and engage one another toward cultivating a literary culture.

This cultivation of literacy and the genius inside these societies perhaps is best exemplified by an excerpt from an 1837 public speech delivered by James Forten (excerpted at left). Forten, a leading thinker, businessman, and social activist, spoke of literary societies in this address. Literary societies were organized reading and writing groups for developing literacy skills, but they also helped members to read, write, and think in ways that would help foster a better humanity for all. These groups were organized as early as 1828 in cities within the northeast region of the United States. These societies existed in major cities such as Philadelphia, New York, and Boston. Black people created their own spaces because they were not invited or allowed to speak or participate in White-run literary organizations. Soon after 1828, other societies spread across the geographic area and developed in cities such as Pittsburgh, Hartford, Washington, D.C., Rochester, and Baltimore. They met regularly in person to discuss literature and to debate. They also communicated with each other and across cities through the use of their pens. Newspapers, pamphlets, and other publications were useful ways to send messages about progress, news of the social times, and updates on their activities. Members paid dues to the societies that went into the cultivation and purchase of books for their libraries. Typically, there were fewer than 10 members who founded individual organizations, but membership in some groups grew to over 100 people.

> *As part of a broader struggle to counter multiple attacks of oppression with violence, they used their minds and pens as weapons to battle injustice.*

Forten's first line in his speech emphasizes that literacy has the power of doing. Literacy is not just about reading words on the page; it also carries some sort of action. In other words, reading and writing are transformative acts that improve self and society. In his speech, Forten called attention to the importance of being able to read, to investigate text, and to teach that no one was created to wear chains of servitude and oppression. He professes that literacy is not just something one attains, but that it is, indeed, a human right.

In contrast to what is currently found in many schools and classrooms, the historical roots of literacy learning in Black communities were much more expansive and advanced and included the goals of identity meaning-making and criticality. In contemporary classrooms across

the nation, teachers, school leaders, and teacher educators are still wrestling with ways to improve and elevate the literacy achievement of youth, especially Black children and other culturally and linguistically diverse populations. Alas, we are underserving large populations of students who are in dire need of excellence, brilliance, and teachers who make it impossible for them to fail. Consider the stagnant achievement over the past 25 years—the result of an overemphasis on skills and drills. Current policies and learning standards that govern schools (such as the Common Core State Standards) are focused primarily on skills and knowledge. We must ask ourselves:

- What is missing from the ways we structure education today?

- Why have school leaders and policy makers been unable to accelerate learning at a greater pace with the standards and pedagogies that have traditionally been taught in schools?

- What is absent from the curricular standards and frameworks that are needed for the holistic development and robust literacy achievement for our children?

- What can we learn from history (particularly Black excellence) to refashion curriculum and instruction today? (Black excellence includes the outstanding attributes and contributions of Black people throughout time and currently, but sadly it is rarely taught in K–12 schools or teacher education programs.)

- Why are school leaders still mandating curricular frameworks that were not explicitly designed for students of color?

If we aim to get it right with all youth, a productive starting point is to design teaching and learning to the group(s) of students who have been marginalized the most in society and within schools. Thus, we need frameworks that have been written by people of color and designed *for* children of color. *Cultivating Genius* provides such a framework.

The model and content of this book puts critical theory, sociocultural theory, and cognitive theories collectively into a practical model for teaching and learning— one that helps youth develop both personally and academically.

In this book, I argue for a reframed set of learning standards in literacy education—one that is grounded in history and that restores excellence in education. These historical learning standards (defined within Historically Responsive Literacy) allow educators to reimagine what learning can look like and begin to offer a promising framework for students who have not traditionally seen themselves in formal learning situations. The framework offered here allows for a practical model based on culturally relevant and responsive theories of education. Further, the model and content of this book puts critical theory, sociocultural theory, and cognitive theories collectively into a practical model for teaching and learning—one that helps youth develop both personally and academically.

From my lenses as a teacher, scholar, school board member, researcher, and teacher educator, I have come to learn that there is much that we can do to improve how literacy education is framed today. In my historical research, I discovered that the ways in which literacy was conceptualized and practiced throughout the 19th century among Black populations were more advanced and, compared to how we engage youth today, more challenging and intellectually invigorating. I sought to understand the lessons educators could learn from our history to then return to this excellence for the sake of our students, teachers, families, and communities. This book was especially written to support those students for whom the educational system was not designed—namely, Black and Brown students. This is the group of students who are most consistently being underserved. My historical inquiry led me to a set of new learning standards to frame goals for literacy education—one that I argue is needed for the current political times and diverse populations of schools. In this book, I share the ways in which literacy was defined historically and offer a four-layered equity framework for reimagining the standards we set for teaching and learning. This practical framework is useful for designing literacy instruction and education across all content areas.

The four-layered equity framework conceptualized here include the learning goals of 1) identity development; 2) skill development; 3) intellectual development; and 4) criticality. Black people who participated in literary societies in Northeastern cities throughout the 19th century, like the one described by James Forten, have held these four goals—or learning pursuits—for personal and academic achievement.

> *Students need spaces to name and critique injustice to help them ultimately develop the agency to build a better world. As long as oppression is present in the world, young people need pedagogy that nurtures criticality.*

I use learning goals and pursuits synonymously to denote the aims we should have for learning. These four learning pursuits defined literacy. And because literacy was synonymous with education during that time, it was also how they framed their general learning. Each time early Black readers came together to read, write, think, and learn, they were making sense of who they were (identity), developing their proficiencies in the content they were learning within (skills), becoming smarter about something or gaining new knowledge and concepts in the world (intellect), and finally, developing the ability to read texts (including print texts and social con-*texts*) to understand power, authority and anti-oppression (criticality). The latter goal of criticality is the capacity to read, write, and think in the context of understanding power, privilege, and oppression. Criticality is also related to seeing, naming, and interrogating the world to not only make sense of injustice, but also work toward social transformation. Thus, students need spaces to name and critique injustice to help them ultimately develop the agency to build a better world. As long as oppression is present in the world, young people need pedagogy that nurtures criticality.

With text at the nexus, this framework helps to redesign the ways in which teacher educators engage preservice teachers at the university level as they prepare the next generation of educators who will serve to disrupt racism, sexism, and other oppressions. This book will help educators redesign their learning goals, lesson/unit plans, and importantly, the texts they use to teach. While offering a space for advanced pedagogy that moves beyond cognitive literacies, the ideas in this book incorporate multiple theoretical orientations to teaching and learning, including cognitive, sociocultural, critical, and sociohistorical theories. Thus, the equity framework discussed in *Cultivating Genius* is named the Historically Responsive Literacy (HRL) Framework, which addresses

students' *Identities, Skills, Intellect,* and *Criticality*. The HRL Framework also responds to the limitations of traditional school curricula, urging us to recognize and embrace the exalted literacy legacy—established by the 19th century Black literary societies—of our students of color.

This historical blueprint is precisely why educators need to move toward *cultivating the genius* that already lies within students and teachers. History from Black communities tells us that educators don't need to empower youth or give them brilliance or genius. Instead, the power and genius is already within them. Genius is the brilliance, intellect, ability, cleverness, and artistry that have been flowing through their minds and spirits across the generations. This cultivation calls for reaching back into students' histories and deeply knowing them and their ancestries to teach in ways that raise, grow, and develop their existing genius. The cultivation of the genius within all of us has been a call throughout history. Alexander Crummell, who was a scholar, teacher, and former Howard University professor, gave a speech entitled *The Attitude of the American Mind Toward the Negro Intellect* [1897]. In the full speech, he noted that those in economic power have never been interested in stimulating the minds of the Black race, which has left Black people alone in many ways. He argues, however, for Black people to stimulate and cultivate their own minds.

Crummell states:

> For the first time in the history of this nation the colored people of America have undertaken the difficult task, of stimulating and fostering the genius of their race as a distinct and definite purpose... To me it is, I confess, a matter of rejoicing that we have, as a people, reached a point where we have a class of men who will come together for purposes, so pure, so elevating, so beneficent, as the cultivation of mind...

This cultivation of the mind or of genius is vital to the success of Black children and, by this model, of all youth.

Genius is the brilliance, intellect, ability, cleverness, and artistry that have been flowing through their minds and spirits across the generations.

In 1837, William Whipper said in a public address, "...as we cultivate our intellectual faculties, we shall strengthen our reasoning powers..." as a goal for education (Woodson, 2015, p. 3).

Not long after, in 1904, Mary Church Terrell wrote about the educational cultivation of Black women and girls and how this effort has yielded academic progress:

> When one considers the obstacles encountered by colored women in their effort to educate and cultivate themselves, since they became free, the work they have accomplished and the progress they have made will bear favorable comparison, at least with that of their more fortunate sisters, from whom the opportunity of acquiring knowledge and the means of self-culture have never been entirely withheld (Mullings & Marable, 2009, p. 166).

To teach geniuses, however, charges teachers to cultivate their own genius that lies within them. A friend told me once that teaching should be reserved for the brightest and most brilliant among us. An anonymous sister author wrote to other sisters of the Philadelphia Literary Association in *The Liberator* newspaper on July 7, 1832, "You have talent—only cultivate them; you have minds—enrich them." If we connect this powerful line to the present moment, teachers need to be truth and knowledge seekers. They must know theory and practice and be masterful with science and the art of pedagogy. African American teacher Prince Saunders supported such efforts in the early 1800s:

> Many, in different periods, by cultivating the arts and sciences, have contributed to human happiness and improvement, by that invincible zeal of moral virtue and intellectual excellence, which their example has inspired in other minds and hearts, as well as by the sublimity of those traces of truth with which they have illuminated the world, and dignified the intercourse of civilized society (Porter, 1995, p. 89).

If teachers do not recognize their own genius, they need to be striving each day for it. Mediocrity is not an option. The Historically Responsive Literacy (HRL) Framework is a universal teaching and learning model that helps teachers cultivate the genius within students and within themselves and teach in ways that create spaces for mutual empowerment, confidence, and self-reliance.

The Historically Responsive Literacy (HRL) Framework is a universal teaching and learning model that helps teachers cultivate the genius within students and within themselves and teach in ways that create spaces for mutual empowerment, confidence, and reliance.

This book is designed for K–12 educators, including teachers, paraprofessionals, and school leaders such as principals, curriculum leaders/writers, and academic coaches. The content in *Cultivating Genius* is also for preservice teachers going into the field and teacher educators as they prepare the next generation of teachers. Finally, it is my hope that those developers and writers behind state standards, district curriculum, and state exams read the four components of the HRL Framework closely as a means to rethink and expand the standards and questions we ask of students.

We have so long prescribed and written what others think is best for youth in schools, all while leaving out of the picture the ways communities of color have historically acquired and used literacy. The culturally and historically responsive literacy framework I offer serves to reorient literacy to our students' lives and asks educators to implement an equity framework that aligns with and accounts for our rich history and exalted literacy legacy.

Drawing From History to Reimagine Literacy Education

Part One of this book introduces the theory and model of Historically Responsive Literacy (HRL) by revisiting the literacy and educational contributions of 19th-century Black literary societies. Lessons from these societies are presented to ground the theory and model of HRL. Contributing to the richness of resource pedagogies (Paris, 2012) and building upon the scholarship of culturally relevant teaching (Ladson-Billings, 1994; 1995), culturally responsive education (Gay, 2000/2010) and other cultural models in education (Lee, 1995; Moll and Gonzalez, 1994; Paris & Alim, 2017), Historically Responsive Literacy is teaching in response to the multiple and cultural histories, identities, and literacy practices of youth. In addition, HRL promotes teaching practices that respond to the sociopolitical times of communities, society, and the world—recognizing that teaching and learning always occur in a socio-cultural-political context.

 **CHAPTER 1**

How 19th-Century Black Literary Societies Can Elevate Today's Literacy Learning

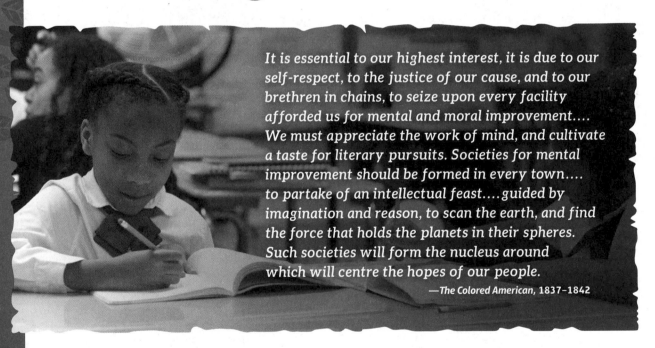

It is essential to our highest interest, it is due to our self-respect, to the justice of our cause, and to our brethren in chains, to seize upon every facility afforded us for mental and moral improvement.... We must appreciate the work of mind, and cultivate a taste for literary pursuits. Societies for mental improvement should be formed in every town.... to partake of an intellectual feast....guided by imagination and reason, to scan the earth, and find the force that holds the planets in their spheres. Such societies will form the nucleus around which will centre the hopes of our people.

—*The Colored American*, 1837–1842

This selection comes from *The Colored American* newspaper, which circulated from 1837 to 1842. The language here introduces the literacy goals of early readers and writers during the 19th century. In this prose, the writer (whose name is not printed due to anonymity and literary protection during hostile times) speaks to his fellow brethren or brothers, pleading for them to seek "mental and moral improvement" by engaging in literary pursuits, reading, thinking, writing, speaking, and debating.

The writer also advocates for fostering a literary society in each town. Black literary societies were built around meaningful and diverse literature and were developed in the early 1800s (McHenry, 2002). Although literacy was the foundation of learning, the groups focused on the study of mathematics, science, history, literature, language, and English. These societies were formed in urban northern cities such as Boston, New York, and Philadelphia, and members came together to read, write, and think. Through the use of powerful language, the writer also compares the meetings of literary societies to an intellectual feast. The fact that the language of food was used to compare the literary benefits one received from membership shows that literacy was tied to nourishment and the essential material for intellectual fulfillment. During these feasts, ideas were discussed freely as they were building political consciousness and intellectualism (McHenry, 2002).

The writer of the newspaper excerpt notes that literacy serves as a form of protection in this world and is rightly guided by both imagination and reason—two constructs that are often dichotomous, especially in current public education. While imagination is praised and cultivated in the early grades, I often find it diminished in middle and secondary schools. Finally, the writer ends with stating that literary societies will be central for the hopes of Black people. Literacy as the hope for Black people was historically steeped into the common narrative of Black literacies. The emancipatory and humanizing aspects of literacy provide access to mental freedom, political power, and agenda building. Literacy also provided the access to navigate extremely racist and oppressive systems and structures of the United States—and schools were one of these systems. Although I don't want to romanticize literacy in any way, nor to imply that literacy resolved racism, literacy gave us a tool to fight back.

I started studying historical literacy development when I began to unearth archives and historical artifacts of Black literary societies throughout the 19th century. I studied primary source documents because I was interested in learning about the ways in which early Black readers and writers defined and practiced literacy across urban contexts of the United States. I engaged in a historical research inquiry (Brettell, 2000; Ramsey, Sharer, L'Eplattenier, & Mastrangelo, 2010), examining 19th-century documents to understand how and why Black people developed literary societies, to what ends these societies were created, and what occurred as a result of their participation. In doing so, I asked questions such as:

- How did these groups define literacy?
- What types of literacy practices existed in the groups?
- What types of text did they read?
- What were their literary pursuits?
- What were the purposes of their literary engagement?
- What were their goals of learning when they came together to read, write, talk, and think?

This inquiry and "archeological dig" led me into the historic archives of newspapers, meeting minutes, announcements, constitutions from literary societies, public addresses by key literary figures, and various literary writings produced by members as a result of their participation. I also relied on the writings of prominent scholars Dorothy B. Porter (1936) and Elizabeth McHenry (2002), as they were instrumental in providing much wider descriptions of societies and the readers who contributed to this rich, yet rarely discussed part of American history. Porter's (1936) work was originally published in the *Journal of Negro Education* and was one of the first studies to outline why literary societies were developed and how they spread across major cities in the United States. Elizabeth McHenry (2002) published her pioneering work, *Forgotten Readers: Recovering the Lost History of African American Literary Societies,* over 60 years later. The emphasis on the name *Forgotten Readers* implies the rarity with which these early readers are discussed or even known. In fact, in my work with educators across the country, very seldom do they have knowledge of this rich sector of American history. This is perhaps due to the oversaturation of the teaching of enslavement or the Civil Rights Movement across K–12 schools. Teachers have largely focused on leading thinkers and activists such as Dr. Martin Luther King Jr. or Rosa Parks and repeatedly start Black people's stories with narratives of struggle or

When we frame the stories of people of color as narratives steeped in pain or even smallness, this becomes the dominant or sole representation.

suffering. This teaching of African American history isn't problematic on its own, but when this becomes the only part of history taught, it is limiting. Chimamanda Ngozi Adichie describes this as the "danger of the single story" (2009). When we frame the stories of people of color as narratives steeped in pain or even smallness, this becomes the dominant or sole representation. In schools today, we often frame Black people's stories with false interpretations, or begin the story with chattel slavery. I see teachers framing students' stories with a school dropout narrative and ignoring what or who may have pushed students out of school. Rarely do young children learn about multiple figures in history who also contributed to excellence—in this case, those who can teach us ways to reframe our current education system.

We have largely withdrawn from the historical excellence of Black education.

In my historical "unearthing" quest, I also aimed to compare historical understandings to the ways in which literacy is defined and practiced across schools today, particularly school communities that have steadily struggled with ways to advance the literacy achievement of Black youth. When considering the rich literacy history of Black Americans, I found that we have retreated in our craft and pedagogical school practices in literacy education. We have progressed toward digital literacies and taken greater strides toward social justice. But we have largely withdrawn from the historical excellence of Black education. While researchers have advanced in telling narratives of excellence in education and outlining what schools and classrooms need, there remains a large gap between what we know *or should know* and what we actually do in classrooms and schools.

Further, one of the largest gaps stems from the theorists who are studied in teacher preparation programs. Rarely do teacher candidates study the educational theories of W. E. B. Du Bois, Anna Julia Cooper, Prince Saunders, Ella Baker, or Carter G. Woodson (to name a few). So, in this book, I intentionally ground literacy learning in Black history and Black excellence as the conduit for framing excellence in education for students across all racial groups, ethnicities, and identities. If we start with Blackness (which we have not traditionally done in schooling) or the group of people who have uniquely survived the harshest oppressions in this country, then we begin to understand ways to get literacy education right for all.

In the following sections, I describe Black literary societies in detail, beginning with how literacy was defined historically and how I define literacy within the context of this book, which is very different from the traditional definition used in schools.

Defining Literacy

Within literary societies, to be educated was to be literate. Literacy among Black people was not just tied to skills and proficiencies, which is a common notion of literacy today, but it was also defined as liberation and power. In this way, literacy was connected to acts of self-empowerment, self-determination, and self-liberation. It is important to note that these were the ambitions they cultivated for *themselves* rather than thinking that others would give them power or determine their life outcomes.

Literacy was connected to acts of self-empowerment, self-determination, and self-liberation.

Literacy was the foundation of all learning. When Black people learned to read, write, and speak, they were able to accumulate knowledge in other areas and use these skills as tools to further shape, define, and navigate their lives. Literacy was not just for self-enjoyment of fulfillment, it was tied to action and efforts to shape the sociopolitical landscape of a country that was founded on oppression. An example of this was using acts of literacy to disrupt racism through their written and spoken words, including public addresses that fostered agitation to shake the wrongdoing placed upon their lives.

A Push for Literacy Amid Racial Hostility

In 1830, when many literary societies took shape, there were 319,599 "free" Black people living in the northern region of the United States. Although they were openly "free," they were frequently subjected to hostility and abuse, and had a number of restrictions placed upon them (McHenry, 2002). In the January 14, 1837 edition of the African American newspaper *Weekly Advocate*, a column entitled "Free Man of Colour" further sheds light on the stigma associated with freedom for African Americans during this period. The author wrote:

> Free Man of Colour.
> What an empty name! what a mockery! Free Man, Indeed! when so unrighteously deprived of every civil and political privilege. Free indeed! when almost every honourable incentive to the pursuit of happiness, so largely and so freely held out to his fairer brother, is withheld from him. A freeman! when prejudice binds the most galling chains around him! drives him from every mechanical employment, and situations of trust, or employment; frowns him from the door of our Institutions of learning; forbids him to enter every public place of amusement, and follows him wherever he goes, pointing at him the finger of scorn and contempt. Is this to be a freeman? Is this to enjoy untrammeled, a freeman's privileges? Is this to be a participant of the freedom of a country boasting to be the freeest under the canopy of Heaven? What a sad perversion of the term freeman!
>
> —*Weekly Advocate*, January 14, 1837

Partaking in the literary tradition of rhetoric, the writer expressed his immense indignation of how the term *free* is loosely applied to Black Americans when, in fact, they were chained by rampant prejudice and completely ignored in the rights outlined in the United States Constitution. The language surrounding freedom as an "empty name" and "mockery," and the association of oppression with freedom exemplifies that Black people were not granted liberation or rights in the true sense of the word.

The political leaders of this time claimed that the United States was the most liberated country in the world, but in truth, the country embodied racial discrimination and enslavement. These conditions, especially in Southern states, restricted Black people from becoming formally educated. Because Black people had limited rights within many social, political, and educational institutions in the United States, they had to rely upon themselves to create and sustain their own organizations and spaces for learning. Rather than wait for their rights and education to be granted from those with legislative power, they instead created their own agendas and claimed authority by organizing into professional associations focused on literacy. Educational spaces included the creation of schools (Anderson, 1988), hush harbors (Kynard, 2010), and benevolent and educational societies (Harris, 1992). Hush harbors were spaces during the antebellum period where Black people gathered in secret for fellowship and religious worship.

In literary societies, members created preambles, constitutions, and thoughtful strategies to move toward actions to improve the minds and hearts of members. The constant blatant racism and "worsening conditions" for African Americans living in Northern cities as "free" people sparked an impulse inside of them to educate themselves, ameliorate the condition of our people, and collaborate to promote change (McHenry, 2002). Prior to literary societies, such organized efforts

included temperance, moral and benevolent coalitions, as well as anti-slavery societies. Within these organizations, Black people were taught self-discipline with a focus on making one's heart open, loving, and pure. In ways, the ideals taught in these spaces served as the roots for building literary societies. Self-discipline was never removed from the ways in which Black people developed and engaged in literacy.

Cultivating the First Black Literary Societies

Other names for literary societies included reading rooms, lyceums, library companies, and debating societies. They were more than just "book clubs" or associations to engage in the study of literature. Instead, they had stronger aims of advancing the conditions of African Americans and others in the wider society. Societies were large and small, and were both gender-specific and unisex, although they initially began solely for males in 1828. Typically, societies under 10 members founded individual organizations, but membership grew to over 100 members in larger organizations. Members of different ages and experiences with literacy gathered around meaningful and significant texts to encourage and improve reading, writing, and speaking skills. They shared knowledge and promoted ideas to cultivate a scholarly and literate way of life (Belt-Beyan, 2004; McHenry & Heath, 1994). In describing these spaces, Belt-Beyan (2004) explains that societies met regularly in basements of churches, buildings with classrooms, libraries, private homes, and auditoriums for events that drew large crowds. They paid dues regularly, which supported texts to furnish libraries and other expenses (Porter, 1936). Engaging in texts led to acts of reading, writing, debating, and speaking, and gave them a means to meet the greater end of elevating their minds and social conditions.

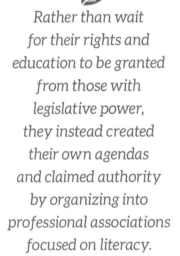

Rather than wait for their rights and education to be granted from those with legislative power, they instead created their own agendas and claimed authority by organizing into professional associations focused on literacy.

In a public address, William Whipper, a businessman and leader of several institutions, pushed for a kind of institution that would cultivate Black males as readers, writers, speakers, and thinkers. Serving as the "guiding spirit" of the group (Porter, 1936), in 1828, Whipper urged his people to work collectively to form a constitution for what would be called "Reading Room Society for Men of Colour" which marked the emergence of one of the earliest Black literary societies. Later Black women created their own spaces, and literary societies also became open for young men and women together. In the same 1828 address before The Colored Reading Society of Philadelphia, Whipper stated:

> It shall be our whole duty to instruct and assist each other in the improvement of our minds, as we wish to see the flame of improvement spreading amongst our brethren, and friends; and the means prescribed shall be our particular province. Therefore

we hope that many of our friends will avail themselves of the opportunity of becoming members of this useful institution (Porter, 1995, p. 108).

The flame metaphorically represented an ideal of shared knowledge and was the core of all efforts of literary societies. Literacy was to be developed in a socially constructed environment so that new ideas and information learned from texts could be shared and spread among one another and those in the community. Members of all ages and experiences with reading would assemble to teach one another. Although individual literacy was valued, these societies were highly collaborative and prompted social responsibility to share knowledge gained from acts of literacy rather than keep education to one's self. This collaboration for literacy learning built the foundation of the "chain letter of instruction" model, which embodied a shared accountability for knowledge (Fisher, 2004). If one person, for example, acquired knowledge, it was then his or her responsibility to pass it on to others to create a flame-like effect. To keep knowledge to one's self was seen as a selfish act, and each person therefore was responsible to elevate others through education in the immediate and larger community. This ideal of collectivism is in direct conflict with schools today, as schools are largely grounded in competition and individualism. This is perhaps one major reason why students of color often do not reach their full potential in schools—because schools are in disharmony with their histories and identities.

> *Although individual literacy was valued, these societies were highly collaborative and prompted social responsibility to share knowledge gained from acts of literacy rather than keep education to one's self.*

Whipper concluded his speech by reiterating the importance for people to exercise their minds and talents through literary means. He emphasized that the exercising of the mind would be applicable in other subjects extended from the *literary* such as science, politics, and history, but in order to meet the greater goal of accumulating such knowledge, they must first build the capacity to receive education. Literary societies became the means to build such capacity.

Historical Framings of Literacy Learning

As I read historical documents, three themes emerged of Black literacy development. These are *literary presence, literary pursuits,* and *literary character*. I refer to these as historical literacy framings because they provided structure and support to build and nurture literacy development in the 1800s and beyond. These frames supported Black people by providing space for their identities and literacies to be valued and honored beyond their physical existence. It is important to note that *literary* was not synonymous with *literacy*. The historical literacy framings concerned the *literary*. In other words, the key to literacy development involved the study, reading, and writing of literary print and literature. This enabled Black people to be established within a literary tradition of written and spoken text.

Literary Presence

Literary presence means staking a claim and making one's self visible within the intellectual community through acts of literacy. Black people did not wish to merely exist in the country; they wanted to exert their presence and make their mark on history in telling their own narratives. They had a thirst to seek new knowledge as well as to be known and recognized for their contributions to scholarship. Members of these societies were keenly aware that this was possible through their writings and public addresses, by educating themselves through literature. Their writings were one major display of literary presence because this would mean their works were accessible for others to read and learn. Literary presence within societies gave them platforms to project their goals and to put their voices on record publicly with goals of having rights granted in larger political, social, educational, and economic contexts.

One way they exerted a literary presence was through their writing and publications. For example, in the October 17, 1840 issue of *The Colored American*, the editor wrote in the Correspondents section, urging other Black men to write for the newspapers to exert their voices, ideas and perspectives. The editor explains that correspondents are too few in number and that there is an urgency to write:

We now call upon those young men, thus having qualified themselves to do good to their brethren, and to help in our elevation, to take up the great questions which be at the foundation of moral elevation, we need not suggest the subjects, they will readily occur to you, and discuss them through the columns of this paper; this is its object and we want help, and every such discussion will have its influence, which cannot be lost.

Our correspondents are too few, when there are so many who ought to write and so much to write about, upon, a case too, so urgent in itself. We call upon our old correspondents who have been silent too long, to wake up, let us hear from you… Brethren let us hear from you, it will make the paper interesting, and interest the people, and do good…

This speaks volumes to the necessity of Black people to have their voices acknowledged and honored.

Literary Presence in the Classroom

1. Create in-school contexts for students to share their voices and visions through acts of reading, writing, and speaking.
2. Select texts that speak to their multiple identities instead of selecting texts based on their reading identities alone.
3. Scaffold ways for students to share their thoughts and respond to texts.

Literary Pursuits

Literary pursuits are specific acts of literacy that are both individual and collaborative. In the most simplistic form, one may think of literary pursuits as literacy activities; however, members of literary societies did not label their endeavors as simple *activities*. Rather, these acts of literacy embodied greater goals and were consequently referred to as *pursuits* that they believed would lead to liberation, self-determination, self-reliance, and self-empowerment. Examples of literary pursuits included reading, discussing issues (often subjects found in texts), giving lectures, offering peer critique on other members' writings, debating, and penning and publishing original writings. As they engaged in literary pursuits, the members of the literary societies surrounded themselves with *enabling texts* for reading, writing, thinking, and debate. Alfred Tatum (2009) describes enabling texts as texts that move beyond a solely cognitive focus such as skill and strategy development, but also have sociopolitical and sociocultural influences. In a historical artifact from the *Weekly Advocate* (renamed *The Colored American* in March of 1837), Samuel E. Cornish explained the purpose of one of the literary pursuits—reading:

> The objects of the institution are general improvement, and training of our youth to habits of reading and reflection.... Many young men, yea! and old ones too, spend their evenings in improper places, because they have no public libraries, no reading rooms, nor useful lectures, to attract their attention, and occupy their leisure hours. We hope to save such from ruin, and lead them to habits of virtue and usefulness...
>
> —*Weekly Advocate*, December 7, 1833

Literary pursuits were enacted simultaneously, so as literary society members were reading, they were also thinking through the text, writing about related topics, and then debating these subjects. These literary pursuits were collaborative, embodied a chain-like effect, and encouraged others to participate.

The enabling texts read and written in literary societies offered a variety of subjects to excite their interests, bring joy and pleasure from reading, and stimulate their minds to think and debate about significant issues. The texts read and written by members included classics from African and English writers, laws of the land, national and international news, letters, maps, sermons, speeches, poetry, narratives, essays, biographies, broadsides, and short stories on literature, science, humanities, and history. It was clear that these texts and the literary pursuits went beyond issues relevant to their local and national contexts, and were responsive to their wider identities.

Literary Pursuits in the Classroom

1. Engage students with texts that create social action and cause them to think differently as a result of what they read.
2. Create an environment that affords students the opportunity to shape their own ideas through acts of literacy.
3. Structure opportunities for critiquing and evaluating what students read and write about within the instruction.

Literary Character

Literary character is the personal and academic characteristics a person developed as a result of their engagement in literary pursuits. The strength of members' personalities and characters was tied to acts of literacy that became absorbed in the lives of Black members. McHenry (2002) describes the development of literary character as the process of accumulating literary skills, which gave "free" African Americans living in the North the means to become exemplary citizens who could participate in the civic life of their communities.

Literary character is the personal and academic characteristics a person developed as a result of their engagement in literary pursuits.

In the May 16, 1840, edition of *The Colored American*, a section entitled "Characteristics of the People of Color—No. 3: Literary Character" was published as the third article in a three-part series about character development of African Americans. The first part discussed religious character, and the second addressed moral character. In the literary character column, the writer, who signed as "Examiner," defined literary character as knowledge gained from literature that created "literary advancement" and improvement of the mind. The writer asserted that literary character can and should be advanced and that no youth or adult should be satisfied with just basic proficiency in reading and writing. Therefore, to have literary character meant to be fully proficient in literacy skills, but it also meant that African Americans were independently able to use literacy tools to project their voices through pursuits associated with print material. Reading, writing, and speaking became a part of their personalities, and they grew to have an appreciation of literature as their lives were defined by acts of literacy.

To have literary character also meant that one was honored and revered within the community because with it came empowerment and a responsibility to serve others. Literary character specifically meant being endowed with self-discipline, intellectual curiosity, civic responsibility, and the ability to use reason, self-expression, eloquence, and agency (McHenry, 2002) through literary pursuits. In many ways, acquiring literary character was the ultimate goal.

For the Colored American
CHARACTERISTICS OF THE PEOPLE OF COLOR—NO. 3.
LITERARY CHARACTER.
While in religion and morals the people of color excel all other classes of the community (as I have feebly endeavored to show by Essays No. 1 and 2,) in literature they are far behind. True, a few possess a taste for literature, and some have made considerable advances in the arts and sciences, but these few are exceptions. The majority have acquired no more than the rudiments of an English education, and the elder portion of our people are content if their children can attain even that; consoling themselves with the idea, that as the limited education they received was sufficient for them, their children must be satisfied with the same advantages; not reflecting that the spirit of the age requires that we should possess more education than they; the progress of our institutions; the advancement of liberal principles; the efforts which are making through the country to unrivet the chains which encircle the limbs of millions of our brethren; the contending opinions as to the means which should be used to accomplish an end so desirable; the acknowledgment, by all, that we now possess mind and soul capable of a higher destiny than slavery; the strong desire evinced by many to elevate us mentally as well as physically—all these, and many more reasons, now require that the present and preceding generations should be more enlightened than our forefathers.

The causes which have tended to produce such opinions, do not now exist, but the effect is still visible in the literary character of the people of color, or rather the want of literary character.

When the principles of slavery were predominant, and when the hypothesis was promulgated that we

Literary Character in the Classroom

1. When literary pursuits are enacted, students will become thinkers and resilient beings.
2. Students will have confidence in reading, writing, and sharing their ideas.
3. This confidence will transfer to other spaces in and out of the classroom.

Ten Lessons From Black Literary Societies

Through my study of African American literary societies, I found 10 central lessons related to literacy instruction. These lessons helped me to understand the ways educators today could use the tenets of Black literary societies to rethink learning in classrooms. These lessons also serve as the prelude of defining Historically Responsive Literacy.

Literacy was viewed as the means of building reading and writing skills and knowledge, as well as the means to shape their identities and critical understandings of themselves, of communities, and of the world.

1. Literacy learning encompassed cognition (reading and writing skills) as well as social and cultural practices (learning about identity and equity).

Literary society members' literacy practices embodied multiple theoretical perspectives to learning. Typically, learning in school classrooms is grounded solely in cognitive perspectives, focusing on skills-based learning. An example of this is teaching only decoding, fluency, and vocabulary in reading instruction, rather than *also* teaching students to know themselves. The sole focus on skills-based learning is also evident by the favoring of high-stakes tests and a heavy reliance on testing data in schools across the nation. When I investigated the theories that framed literacy learning in literary societies, I found that multiple perspectives shaped their engagement in literacy development, including critical theories, social learning theories, and cognition. Literacy was viewed as the means of building reading and writing skills and knowledge as well as the means to shape their identities and critical understandings of themselves, of communities, and of the world.

2. Literacy was the foundation and was central to all disciplinary learning.

Historically, literacy was the root of all education including learning in the academic discipline areas of mathematics, science, and history. Literary societies focused on literacy development but were grounded in the learning of the disciplines. Society meetings were not linear in their studies, and the literacy often enabled interdisciplinary understandings. This way of learning differs from classrooms today that oftentimes lack a literacy focus in the academic content areas of science, math, and social studies.

3. Literacy learning involved print and oral literacy, and these were developed simultaneously.

In most schools today, reading, writing, and language are different classes. Typically, youth learn language and writing in one class and reading and literature in another. Language development is also typically developed in the framework of grammar instruction rather than reading literature and within students' own writings (Diamondstone, 2002; Zuidema, 2012). This was not a historical practice in literary societies. A tradition among Black people involved the cultivation of reading, writing, and oral literacies together, layered upon their contextual readings of the world. I found that the literary pursuits in societies involved reading, writing, and debating on popular topics of the time, and offered lectures on the topics they read and wrote about (McHenry, 2002).

4. Literacy instruction was responsive to the social events and people of the time.

Researchers who study and write about culturally relevant and responsive instruction among African Americans (Gay, 2010; Ladson-Billings, 1994) find that the education of Black people has traditionally been connected to their histories and identities. Oftentimes, when Black readers of the 19th century engaged in literacy learning, it called for them to not just read printed text but to also read their social world (Freire & Macedo, 1987). The social environment especially dictated the topics they chose to read, write, and speak about.

5. Literacy was tied to joy, love, and aesthetic fulfillment.

I find that schools educating students of color often focus on rote, linear, and prescriptive teaching practices. In the midst of this, the learning content oftentimes neglects to teach them to experience joy and contentment in literature and learning as teachers are often pressured to raise test scores. Yet, I found that even within social and political tumult, Black people still

Through their reading and writing, they still practiced joy and cultivated love.

engaged in literacy practices to both improve their hearts as well as their aesthetic sensibility toward education. In other words, through their reading and writing, they still practiced joy and cultivated love.

6. Learners of different literacies and experiences came together to learn from one another—using each other's ways of knowing as resources for new learning.

It was an intentional practice to galvanize young people of different ages and "abilities" in literacy together. Cornelius (1983) notes from her historical research on enslavement and literacy processes from 1830 to 1865 that it was a practice for brothers and sisters who were enslaved to learn how to read and subsequently teach one another. Also, other family members, young and old, would teach one another. This was viewed in the common landscape of educational and literary societies. Although most school classrooms today are organized by students' ages and reading abilities, this practice was not common historically. It was a practice, however, to use others' experiences and abilities as resources to teach and learn from one another.

7. Literacy learning was highly collaborative, and a shared learning space was created.

Rather than learning being competitive and individualistic, it was collaborative and socially constructed. Learners had a social responsibility to one another. This is completely the opposite of what I find in classrooms today where students are rarely encouraged to construct knowledge together in ways in which they become responsible for each other's academic growth.

8. Literacy learning involved reading and writing diverse text genres and authorship.

Members of literary societies did not limit their reading and writing to one particular genre, author, or form of text. Instead, they read across a range of diverse subjects and authorship. They read Black writers as well as authors from around the globe. In societies, they also read and wrote cross-genre texts including poetry, essays, speeches, articles, pamphlets, travel logs, and other literature.

9. Literacy learning also focused on how to reclaim the power of authority in language through critical literacy.

To claim the authority of language, one had to read with a critical lens (Schiller, 2008). Members of literary societies' writings, for example, became transcriptions of resistance. Language was the means to assert one's existence as well as one's voice and stance on political issues. Literacy was always connected to social justice and change for the rights of humanity. Using language to engender trust and support of readers while disseminating important knowledge reflected the authority African Americans claimed over print.

10. Identity and intellectual development were cultivated alongside literacy learning.

Identity and intellect were two important facets to literacy learning. In other words, as Black people read and wrote, they often did so to make sense of their individual and collective identities as Black people while also gaining new knowledge. Although knowledge development is outlined in state standards across the nation, there is an absence of a discussion about identity.

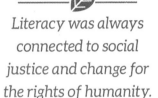

Literacy was always connected to social justice and change for the rights of humanity.

I use these lessons of literary societies as the means to begin to reframe literacy education for youth today, especially as we consider how most schools are currently grounded in standardized one-size-fits-all models and curricula frameworks that are not designed with youth of color in mind. This becomes apparent when we consider the emphasis educators place on large-scale assessments. What's more, cultural models such as culturally responsive education often appear to be an "add-on" in schools and districts rather than the means of framing systems. These problems within education and the ahistorical nature of teaching youth of color created the need to reframe and historicize learning today.

Literary Societies and Literacy Elevation

In a call for a convention of literary societies of the Banneker Institute, it was proclaimed:

> There can be no more effective manner of elevating our people than by a spread of literature, and no more speedy way of demonstrating to those in authority in our government that we are susceptible of the highest degree of mental culture and worthy of the rights which have been so long withheld from us.

This very powerful statement brings me back to one of my initial questions: What larger goal propelled Black people to create literary societies to project their voices (literary presence), engage in acts of literacy (literary pursuits), and develop the character connected to their literacy development (literary character)? From the archival evidence, *elevation* meant improvement and advancement in mental development. They

simultaneously cultivated their minds so that they would be in higher positions to advocate for their rights and create the capacity to provide a better future for Black people throughout the country.

The three historical literacy framings, along with the lessons of literary societies, worked collectively to advance literacy development. Working in tandem, each served a unique purpose in giving early readers and writers the means and tools to sustain themselves and protect the rights and voices of future generations. The enactments of the historical literacy framings afforded readers with the opportunity to develop a sense of self and agency while claiming the authority of their rights. This historical narrative sharply contrasts with what I see in schools today. Specifically, there is a lack of attention in research, policy, and practice given to how communities of color have historically developed literacy and how elements of these historical findings can be transferred into contemporary spaces that serve to educate youth. Historically Responsive Literacy (HRL) consequently begins to connect the excellence of the past to the current educational landscape of schools and classrooms. As a theory and model, HRL begins to follow the road map established by the early Black literary societies. HRL will help educators work to rebuild frameworks for the present and future.

Questions for Further Consideration: Teachers and Preservice Teachers

1. What are your own ideologies and beliefs? What are your own learning goals in your classroom?
2. How is literacy defined in your classroom?
3. Does literacy learning focus on skills only or also on wider goals?
4. How are literary presence, literary pursuits, and literary character observed in your classroom?
5. How do the 10 lessons from literary societies compare with pedagogy in your classroom?

Questions for Further Consideration: Principals and School Leaders

1. What are your own beliefs about teaching and learning? What are your own learning goals in your school?
2. How is literacy defined at the school and district levels? Does it focus on skills only or wider goals?
3. How are literary presence, literary pursuits, and literary character observed in schools?
4. How do the 10 lessons from literary societies compare with policies and norms of the district? Think about the norms, policies, and goals for curriculum and instruction for classrooms and schools with the district. How are teachers encouraged to teach?
5. How do professional development and teacher evaluation support the lessons from Black literary societies?

CHAPTER 2

What Is Historically Responsive Literacy?

> It has been most happily said, by one of the greatest of modern philosophers, that "Knowledge is power;" and never has the excellency of its possession been doubted by the candid and liberal; but education must begin in youth, in order to furnish men of erudition. Our youth are the men of a coming age; and who can calculate the importance of competent instruction in the development of their powers, and in the formation of their minds. How many millions are ruined in their early days, for the want of good instruction! Yes! We need to be constantly reminded of the power of education, right or wrong, thorough or superficial, controlled or slighted—to make or ruin the hopes of our country; and in reference to this subject, it has been said, with propriety, that a man cannot leave his country a better legacy than a well-educated family.
>
> —**Robert Sears**

This stirring quote by Robert Sears, a White contributor who often critiqued the current state of politics and education in the United States, was originally published July 8, 1837, in *The Colored American* newspaper. Sears argued that a quality education and quality of life are intertwined human rights and must be both excellent and powerful. For decades, communities of color especially have been resisting wrongful, deficit-based education. Indeed, we have worked to name and describe the education we deserve to avoid the ruin of poor education.

Cultural Theories and Models

From her work with successful teachers of African American students, Gloria Ladson-Billings coined the term *culturally relevant education*. Following the ancestors' examples, Ladson-Billings named and described the type of education African American students deserved. She defined culturally relevant education as a "theoretical model that not only addresses student achievement, but also helps students to accept and affirm their cultural identity while developing critical perspectives that challenge inequities that schools (and other institutions) perpetuate" (1995, p. 469). At this time, culturally relevant education was seen as a theory for reframing education to not only structure learning to be more identity-centered, but also to focus on sociopolitical learning in student achievement.

Marginalization and Other Challenges

The need for culturally relevant education stemmed from the multiple ways Black children and other youth with "kindred struggles" (Johnston, D'Andrea Montalbano & Kirkland, 2017) were marginalized and treated poorly in schools. In fact, when I examined research related to the literacy development of Black girls and boys over the past 25 years, I (along with co-researchers) found the following:

- The nation's educators still struggle with how to advance the literacy development of Black boys and girls.
- The reading performance of middle and high school–aged Black children has remained relatively flat since the 1980s due to instruction and other factors.
- Black girls are often negatively represented in and out of schools, and the focus has been on their behavior, not their academic aptitude.
- Black girls are among the highest-growing populations of incarcerated youth.
- There are several influences shaping their academic trajectories in the categories of instructional (skills and strategies), sociocultural (home environment and access to economic, human, and

community resources), and personal (confidence, individual attributes) factors.

- Instruction is largely ahistorical—that is, the ways people of color have excelled in literacy historically are absent from the ways educators engage them in instruction today (Tatum & Muhammad, 2012; Muhammad & Haddix, 2016).

Additionally, there is a growing mismatch of incoming teachers and students. Teachers are largely White, female, and monolingual, while classrooms are increasingly multilingual and multi-ethnic (Zumwalt & Craig, 2005). This does not mean that these teachers cannot teach Black and Brown students excellently, but it means that work needs to be done to learn and respond to the social and cultural lives of students.

This work is often beyond what most teacher preparation programs offer. Such programs generally do not ground teacher preparation in Black or cultural studies. Nor do most teacher preparation programs centralize anti-racism, anti-oppression, or learning about Black educational history or Black learning theorists. In fact, we too often see "diversity" or "multicultural" classes as isolated efforts rather than grounding entire programs in intersectionality as we see in Black and cultural studies programs. Urban education courses will have classes related to poverty before having a class centered on Black and Brown excellence. Ironically, an urban education class on poverty doesn't capture the current nature of urban cities across the U.S. as many people of color are being pushed out of urban areas due to gentrification. If we as a nation are struggling to "get it right" with Black and Brown student populations, shouldn't we ground teacher preparation in the essence of Black and cultural learning theories and practices? Instead, again and again, I find that curricular mandates in our nation's largest school districts are often written and guided by Whiteness and lack education that teaches youth to be socially and politically conscious beings—which are intelligences that they need to survive and thrive during and after K–12 education (Love, 2019).

Deficit Language

Another problem that led to the need for culturally relevant education is the deficit language surrounding the lives of children of color—language such as *at risk, defiant*, and *disadvantaged*. More recent policies and programs such as Response to Intervention continue to perpetuate inadequate thinking about young people of color, giving them labels such as "red group" or "tier 3." These labels also connect to naming youth as "non-readers," or "struggling readers." In a statement of culturally responsive education, Johnston, D'Andrea Montalbano & Kirkland (2017) stated: "The creation and assignment of such labels separates students into those who are alienated from their identities and those alienated from education as unuseful, unproductive, or likely unsuccessful, and they are further told similar messages of inadequacy and undesirability in media and society" (p. 18). This speaks to the harmful consequences of such labels for youth and their lives. Students may struggle in reading print, but it should not be the central ways in which they are defined.

Many times, youth may struggle with skills like decoding or reading fluency, but they can read social contexts and environments exceptionally well. They can read teachers' moods and temperaments and if they feel the teachers like them or not. They become very skilled at reading people, expressions and dispositions. This type of reading shouldn't go unacknowledged, especially since this *sociocultural reading* of contexts and people have historically counted as reading among Black people. In truth, this contextual reading led many enslaved people to gaining freedoms.

The problems leading to the need for culturally relevant education have been inadequately addressed by many policies and initiatives in education. These become fresh coats of paint on structures that are debilitating.

While the look of these new approaches may seem different and innovative, they are not. They are just masking the same systemic ways of being and thinking about learning. These approaches continue to marginalize those who are already underserved in and out of schools. Examples of this "repainting," to name a few, are evident in No Child Left Behind, Response to Intervention, and Race to the Top. More recently the College Board announced the "adversity score" for the SAT, which doesn't get to the root of the problem with inequities and testing bias. These have been promoted under the guise of true equity, but they have instead either perpetuated harm on their own or, at best, failed to attack the root of the problem. Further, critical theorists of color are not largely the authors of these initiatives.

Culturally Relevant Education

Ladson-Billings made quite a mark on educational research and pedagogical practice because she began to put a name to the practices Black people have engaged in from the moments they were forcibly brought to the United States until contemporary times. Culturally relevant education (although not yet named) can be found in African philosophies of education, Black-centered schools in the United States, practices in Black literary societies, directions for education in Civil Rights and Black Power movements, and scholarship from authors such as Anna Julia Cooper, Mary McLeod Bethune, Carter G. Woodson, and W. E. B. Du Bois. This certainly is not an exhaustive list but begins to signify that Black people throughout history have laid the groundwork for education for all. I also found in a December 1, 1969 article in the *Black News* newspaper a list of 15 demands by Black high school students. These demands included:

1. No more automatic suspension of high school students

2. No more police or police aides inside NYC schools

3. Strict adherence to fire regulations—doors to schools must be left open

4. Open the schools daily to parent observation

5. Community rehabilitation centers must be allowed to set up programs to treat known drug addicts in the school buildings

6. Elimination of the General Course of Study

7. Elimination of all Regents Exams

8. Recognition in all NYC schools of two Black Holidays: May 19 (Malcolm X's birthday) and January 15 (Martin Luther King Jr.'s birthday)

9. Immediate alternation of teacher population and examinations to supply Black educators proportionate to the student population

10. Complete examination of all books and educational supplies and materials used by the schools to their adequacy and relevancy

11. The creation of school clubs along ethnic lines with facilities and funds from the G.O.

12. Improved conditions for the students in the schools, such as music in the lunchrooms, more dances, improved athletic programs, and self-defense classes

13. Teachers with a background related to the course they are teaching

14. Creation of Student Faculty Council (equal representation), in each school which will make decisions on the following matters: curriculum, school staff, discipline, rules and regulations, etc.

15. The reorganization of the high schools along community lines so that Black students will not be forced to go to schools in hostile communities and seek an education

Threaded throughout these demands is the naming and demand for culturally relevant education spoken by youth. Using their minds and pens as a form of literary activism, they demand systems, structures, curriculum, and instruction that is connected to their lives and the sociopolitical nature of the community. Number 10 especially called for a review and examination of educational materials for the relevancy to the identities of students. This is yet another historically documented example of Black people calling for culturally relevant education. Other demands teach educators that if we just listen to the voices of youth, we will know exactly what to do in solving the problems in education. Their statements spoke to the need to have teaching, learning, and schooling be responsive to their histories, identities, literacies, and times in which they live.

Using their minds and pens as a form of literary activism, they demand systems, structures, curriculum, and instruction that is connected to their lives.

Connecting Instruction to Students' Cultural Identities and Practices

Carrying the words of the youth and of Black history, Ladson-Billings' work informed educators of the importance of designing curriculum and instructional practices that authentically connect to students' cultural identities and cultural practices. Teachers were encouraged to incorporate students' cultures into their teaching as assets to classroom instruction rather than deficits to overcome (Paris, 2012). Culture is such a broad term, but has been defined as shared and common beliefs, models for living, and practices by a group of people. Cultural relevance is equity-centered and charges educators to engage in practices that push for social justice. Ladson-Billings (2014) concluded three major domains of the successful teachers' work:

1. *Academic Success* or the intellect students gain as result of classroom instruction and learning

2. *Cultural Competence* or the ability to help students appreciate and celebrate their cultures of origin while gaining knowledge of and fluency in at least one other culture

3. *Sociopolitical Consciousness* or the ability to take learning beyond the confines of the classroom using school knowledge and skills to identify, analyze, and solve real-world problems (p. 75)

Following this, in her 2000 text entitled *Culturally Responsive Teaching: Theory, Research, and Practice,* Geneva Gay elaborates on the term "cultural responsiveness." She defines culturally responsive teaching as "using the cultural characteristics, experiences, and perspectives of ethnically diverse students as conduits for teaching them more effectively" (Gay, 2002). Her premise rests on the philosophy that teachers can't teach until they deeply know and understand cultural and ethnic ways of knowing and being, and this includes the tools, protocols, values, traditions, and ways of living of the students they teach. Gay (2010) suggests that students' interest and engagement in learning increase when educators use pedagogies connected to their experiences. Additionally, teachers using this approach see curriculum as a tool of power and a disruption of marginalization. In contrast, when students in classrooms do not receive such curriculum with elements of care, love, and respect at the center, they tend to display resistance to the curriculum and instruction, as well as to teachers and to the school (Johnston, D'Andrea Montalbano & Kirkland, 2017). This resistance is usually called defiance and negative behavior in schools today. I want to remind readers of three moments in history when youth have resisted curriculum and instruction that lacked equity, access, and cultural relevance. They were consequently called defiant.

Picture #1—In the 1970s in South Africa, this photo displays Black children resisting Bantu education, which had substandard curriculum and resources in South Africa. They were also forced to learn in the Afrikaans language (which the youth called the oppressor's language), which was a language not spoken in the homes and communities of indigenous Africans.

Picture #2—In this photo, elementary-aged Black children are being taken to jail on May 4, 1963, after their arrest for protesting segregation in the United States.

Picture #3—In this photo from the 1960s, there is protest by young people resisting an education that didn't give them proper books and instruction.

What is common among all three historical photos is that when we look at them today, we speak of the students' bravery and courage to organize in ways to interrupt wrongdoing. Black students today don't receive that same commentary, yet they are in similar ways resisting curriculum and instruction that were not designed to advance their academic success or personal achievement.

Culture-Centered Theories and Models

In the midst of Ladson-Billings and Gay's work, other researchers have contributed to the educational community with other culture-centered theories and models. These include but are not limited to:

- **Funds of Knowledge** (Moll & Gonzalez, 1994) Using students' reserves of knowledge constituted by events and activities of their households and communities to teach them
- **Cultural Modeling** (Lee, 1995) A framework for instruction that leverages everyday knowledge of youth

- **Culturally Sustaining Pedagogies** (Paris, 2012) "Seeks to perpetuate and foster—to sustain—linguistic, literate, and cultural pluralism as part of the democratic project of schooling" (Paris, 2012, p. 95)

> Historically Responsive Literacy is when teaching, learning, and leadership beliefs and practices authentically respond to:
> 1. Students' cultural (and other) identities
> 2. The cultural (and other) identities of others
> 3. The social times (historical and current)

Historically Responsive Literacy aligns with these models of "responsiveness" and "relevancy" as well as other cultural models in education, but is more pointedly centered on the literacy histories of Black people and a practical framework that teachers can use to guide and shape instruction. The emphasis on literacy and history is key because literacy is something that is practiced and developed across all educational learning and content areas. Thus, HRL becomes both a theory and a model that can be put into action in schools and classrooms. While a theory helps educators to explain or understand phenomena observed

in schools related to teaching and learning, a model serves as a metaphor to represent and explain a theory (Alvermann, Ruddell, & Unrau, 2013). A model represents a theory's variables and focuses more on the practicality of a theory. I frequently hear that teachers and school leaders understand culturally relevant/responsive education as a theory and understand its meaning. Yet, when it comes to putting this theory into accessible instructional and leadership actions, there is confusion about what to do exactly. I respond to this need to place theory into action and to pragmatize research through a four-layered pedagogical model.

Historically Responsive Literacy: Responding to the Histories, Identities, Literacies, and Language Practices of Students

Historically Responsive Literacy authentically draws upon and responds to the histories, identities, and literacy and language practices of students for teaching and learning:

- *Histories* include students' family, local, national, and global histories. Current instruction to culturally and linguistically diverse youth is often ahistorical and absent of the ways diverse groups have historically practiced and conceptualized literacy practices.

- *Identities* are multilayered and shaped by the social and cultural environment as well as by literacy practices (Gee, 2000). Examples of identities include racial, ethnic, cultural, gender, kinship, academic/intellectual, personal/individual, and community. Oftentimes, schools focus on students' perceived racial and gender identities and discount the other ways they self-identify. Students need opportunities in literacy pedagogy to explore multiple facets of self-identity and to learn about the identities (including cultural identities) of others who are different from them. Through the developmental years, young people are constantly understanding and (re)making a sense of positive selfhood. This is especially important for culturally and linguistically diverse youth who have a history of being negatively represented and marginalized across large public platforms, including media and schools. To combat this, students need opportunities in class to make sense of their lives so that others cannot tell their stories.

- Finally, HRL takes a multiple *literacies* and *language* perspective and moves beyond the emphasis of defining literacy as solely reading, writing, and language skills. Instead, this approach takes a multiliteracies approach to underscore an understanding of literacies as being layered, nuanced, and complex. If literacy practices in classrooms are multiple and diverse, then students have a greater potential to achieve both personally and academically, especially within reading development (Moje, Luke, Davies & Street 2009). HRL responds to students' multiple literacy and languages practices. This includes the ways they read, write, speak, and know the world.

Historically Responsive Literacy builds upon the historical literacy practices of Black communities from the 19th century onward. Within an HRL approach, the ideologies, language used, instructional materials, and instructional practices honor and are authentically responsive to students' histories, identities, and literacies (which includes the ways

they use language). The social and political environment shapes students' histories, identities, and literacies and therefore they are always in flux and constantly changing. In this way, pedagogy must be viewed as both an art (imagination and creativity) and a science (theory, strategies, and methods of instruction). This approach calls for teachers to first unpack and make sense of their own histories and identities, which includes the ways they have used language and literacy practices in their own lives. In doing so, they must also unpack their own biases, assumptions, racisms, and other oppressive thoughts they have come to believe about people of color or other people whom others have marginalized.

Approaches for Learning and Understanding the Histories, Identities, and Literacies of Students

Questions for Learning Students' Histories

- What are the histories of my students' schooling/school experiences?

- What are the histories of my students' families/cultures?

- What are the histories of our students' wider histories in their communities, in society, and in the world? Who are their people? How did they practice literacy and language historically?

Questions for Learning Students' Identities

- What are ways in which my students see and define their own lives?

- How are my students defined by others (both positive and negative representations)? If negative, how can we provide learning spaces to name, critique, and push back against such views? If positive, how can we provide learning spaces to help them trust and believe in the ways others see them?

- Whom do my students desire to be in their future? How do my students see their most desired future versions of themselves? How can my classroom instruction enable and cultivate these identities?

Questions for Learning Students' Literacy and Language Practices

- How do my students practice literacies at home and in their communities? What language(s) do they speak?

- What is the purpose of literacy and language in their lives?

- How were literacy and language cultivated historically with their families and ancestors?

In general, I suggest that educators to do the following:

- **Listen to and trust the child.** This seems like such a simple approach, but it is surprising how many people dismiss the ideas, perspectives, and opinions of people of color and of children— as if they are not being fully transparent about their experiences.

- **Engage in teacher action research.** Teachers engage in inquiry-based learning and assessments of their own practices. Ethically, they seek knowledge about their students and about their pedagogy.

- **Ask students to write their autobiographies and personal narratives.** Students can start with their earliest memories of traditions, education, religion, triumphs, defeats, and so on. Teachers must have permission to read such personal accounts. Teachers may also engage students in digital storytelling to depict their own lives and create a multimodal presentation.

- **Interview parents or family members of students who are culturally different from them.** Invite family and community members to the school to hear and learn for them.

- **Study the curriculum and explore ways to make studies meaningful to students and their families and communities.** Too often educators passively follow curriculum and standards that were not designed with their students in mind. Rather, we need to analyze and criticize what we are told to teach and what we are told to teach with. Then, educators should add to the existing curriculum to authentically teach in HRL ways.

Historically Responsive Literacy: Responding to the Social Times (Historically and Currently)

Historically Responsive Literacy also calls for educators to be responsive to the social and political times we have historically lived in and currently live within. When working directly with teachers, I often ask, *How would you describe our social times (historical or current)?* Regularly, I hear responses like, "dismal, hopeless, tragic, racist, sexist, and lacking compassion for people who are oppressed like Black folks, immigrants, and Muslims"; other descriptions might include "technological, forward thinking, and more access to information." HRL practices are responsive to all of the above and additionally include engaging in literacy practices that are multimodal and digital while also teaching and learning how to respond to racism, religious discrimination, homophobia, sexism, ableism, classism, and other oppressions.

The critical need for a culturally responsive pedagogy is best exemplified when we connect the past to the present and witness the lack of progress we have made as a country. For example, in my historical work, I found an excerpt from an 1896 Black newspaper, which describes police brutality when a sheriff fired shots into a crowd of Black boys, killing one and wounding others. The sheriff claimed the order came in to shoot over their heads to frighten them.

Negro Boys Shot In Florida

PENSACOLA, Fla., Apr. 25, 1896—A sheriff's posse brutally fired into a crowd of colored boys, killing one and wounding several others. The boys were practicing military movements.

The sheriff is said to have ordered the posse to frighten the boys by shooting over their heads. But in the gunfire, one boy was killed and several wounded. Commenting on the incident, the black editor of the *Richmond Planet* asked: "Will the day ever come when white men in the South will cease their inhumanity to Negroes?"

One Black commentator added: *Will the day ever come when white men in the South will cease their inhumanity to Negroes?* Fast-forward 116 years later when we witnessed the murder of 17-year-old Trayvon Martin by George Zimmerman. We are still asking the same questions about the senseless killing of our children. We are still hearing poor and unjust excuses for killing (physically and spiritually) Black children. This is just one example of the oppression, and we know that films and TV shows, commercial ads, literature, and other media have conditioned us to accept these.

I am also reminded of countless racist and sexist advertisements historically (and presently) that have represented Black and Brown people as unintelligent, unattractive, and uncouth, while women were depicted as subservient and unable to work. And because we know that schools reflect society, we have police roaming school hallways and policing classrooms, Black teens arrested for infractions that White students escape with only a slap on the wrist, and Black teens being tried as adults. Whiteness pervades nearly everything from nursery rhymes, cartoons, children's literature in the Common Core State Standards, and the ways in which we interact with and teach our students.

The news brings reports of children of color facing mental and physical abuse in schools or encountering educators who devalue their worth and potential. And the texts teachers are given also undermine the heritage and cultural identities of children of color. Textbooks are still not written to give a complete account of Black lives or the history of enslavement. Less than 25 percent of children's books in the past 18 years contain multicultural content—the majority not created by authors of color. Most schools desire culturally responsive practices without deep conversations about the root cause of this theory and model. The need for Culturally Relevant Education (CRE) and Historically Responsive Literacy (HRL) is clear—racism and the dehumanizing of Black people in and outside of schools. This is why HRL specifically calls for urgent pedagogies that are not just responsive to the social times but pedagogies that are anti-racist and overall, anti-oppressive.

Historically Responsive Literacies Call for "Urgent Pedagogies"

I argue that what is (still) needed is a shift. A shift in thinking and the types of instructional practices in which we engage our young people, a shift in the policies that govern the schools, a shift in the curriculum that teachers are told to teach, and a shift in the ways we support and prepare teachers for the field. We live in a period where there's no time for "urgent-free pedagogy." Our instructional pursuits must be honest, bold, raw, unapologetic, and responsive to the social times. This message is embodied in a 1967 interview with Gwendolyn Brooks (Gayles, 2003). At one point in time, Brooks was known for writing sonnets and "lighter" poems about love.

Brooks' love poetry embodied the essence and purity of love, but in the late 1960s she was asked about the shift in her writings when she moved to write more about Black ideology and expression. She was asked if she was still writing sonnets. She responded:

No, I'm not writing sonnets, and I probably won't be, because,
as I've said many times, this does not seem to me to be
a sonnet time. It seems to be a free verse time, because this is
a raw, ragged, uneven time—with rhymes, if there are rhymes,
incidental and random. I am in transition (Gayles, 2003, p. 68).

From the times that Black people were stolen away into slavery until
today, we have been in transition. Transition typically signifies change,
development, and transformation. Transitions are challenging, and diverse
people have always lived in a
transitional state due to the social
environment and the times that
have not always been kind and
fair. We have had to resist and live
in a constant state of resistance
or transition. We are still living
in uneven times; traditional
forms of pedagogy and research
are not warranted. We need
raw and historic pedagogies—
and responsiveness. We need
excellence in schools that helps to
advance marginalized communities
so that young people can rise up
and experience joy and love and
the rich learning they deserve.
How do we engage youth in
schools? How do we engage them
in reading, writing, speaking, and thinking practices in pedagogies that are
responsive to the social times and responsive to the social, cultural, ethnic,
and gendered identities of our youth? How do teachers, the curriculum
and instruction, and school leadership serve to disrupt racism, sexism, and
other oppressions? What critical issues warrant the urgency of students'
pens, learning, and thinking? The Historical Responsive Literacy model
begins to answer these questions.

Examples of Urgent Pedagogies

- Using diverse forms of text by diverse authors
- Harnessing positive energy to push through weariness
- Building collaborative curriculum with youth
- Teaching in ways that move beyond sanctioned norms and processes
- Listening to students of color even when you don't agree or understand
- Making it impossible for students to fail
- Writing and reflecting on teaching practices
- Teaching in unapologetic ways
- Decentering self as the teacher
- Becoming a scholar of the discipline you teach and knowing the meaning and histories of your content areas

Historically Responsive Literacy Calls for Knowledge of:

- Self and our own ideologies
- Culture and identity
- Our students' lives
- Our historical and current social times
- History and the authentic histories of our content areas
- Instructional methods of responsive pedagogy
- A natural sense of imagination, innovation and artistic sensibilities of teaching

Students carry rich experiences and ways of knowing, speaking to, and being in the world. In order to teach in HRL ways, teachers must spend time cultivating the mind (their intellect), the heart (how they feel about youth), and the hands (strategies and methods craft of teaching). When teachers ask immediately for the strategies, I know they haven't first cultivated their thinking and love for this work and the students they teach.

The Historically Responsive Literacy Model: Identity, Skills, Intellect, and Criticality

As I investigated historical records, literacy and responsive education across Black literary communities were largely conceptualized in four ways—as identity development, skills development, intellect, and criticality. These four goals or pursuits connected to the body of literacy research on cognitive and sociocultural perspectives of literacy development and what youth need to attain personal and academic success. It's key to remember that literacy was synonymous with education, so although I name "literacy," these four pursuits can be used and layered with math, science, ELA, social studies, or physical education/health.

1. Literacy as Identity Meaning-Making

While historic Black communities in literary societies read and wrote texts, they also defined literacy as the ability to read and write their lives (Freire & Macedo, 1987). The ability to read one's world meant understanding the self within local and broader contexts and reading the signs of the time to inform their actions and behaviors. They were able to make meaning of their many and complex identities including their collective Black identity in America to their larger global identities and positions in the world. The topics and texts selected for study held themes that supported defining their lives and helped them to gain confidence in knowing who they are.

2. Literacy as Skills

Aligned with traditional definitions, literacy was identified as cognitive acts of reading, writing, and speaking skills—as being able to read and write print independently. Finding meaning in language and the construction of meaning was the central goal for their literacy development. Learning and practicing acts of reading, writing, and speaking would lead members to experience joy in literature and give them a platform to project their voices to public audiences. They also learned skills necessary across other content areas.

3. Literacy as <u>Intellect</u>

Literacy was viewed as an intellectual endeavor. As they were reading, writing, and speaking, they were doing so to gain new academic knowledge. Acts of literacy were tied to the historical tradition of scholasticism during this time (Kallus & Ratliff, 2011) and they were gaining knowledge across disciplinary areas. Literacy development was the root of all other learning in the disciplines including literature, language, science, history, and mathematics.

4. Literacy as <u>Criticality</u>

An end goal of literacy entailed a transformative purpose for change and liberation. In this way, literacy was also a step toward social change and linked to the ideals of liberation, security, and protection. Acts of reading, writing, and speaking served both oppressive and emancipatory functions in the 19th century (Harris, 1992). Because rights were denied and the ideologies of those in legislative power neglected to fully represent the rights and presence of Black people, they began to use literacy as the means to counter injustice and misrepresentations. Gaining authority over print meant that they did not wait or seek permission from others to use language in ways to infuse their own voices, ideals, and stances.

As teachers think of these four pursuits in their HRL instruction, they should ask themselves:

- **Identity:** How will my instruction help students to learn something about themselves and/or about others?
- **Skills:** How will my instruction build students' skills for the content area?
- **Intellect:** How will my instruction build students' knowledge and mental powers?
- **Criticality:** How will my instruction engage students' thinking about power and equity and the disruption of oppression?

I argue that young people in classrooms today need teaching and learning opportunities to cultivate these four pursuits and learning goals. These four ways of conceptualizing literacy become the four-layered equity framework and begin to take culturally responsive theory and put it into a practical model that teachers can take up in classrooms across content areas. The Historically Responsive Literacy Framework is a set of interdisciplinary learning goals for rethinking and redesigning curriculum and pedagogy. The identity and criticality elements of the HRL Framework also help to differentiate between good teaching and responsive teaching. In other words, good teaching may just be the teaching of skills and intellect, but historically responsive literacy teaching is the teaching of all four.

Still, we have to ask what happens when we just teach one or two of the four goals. When studying several states' learning goals, I find they are either focused solely on skills or on skills and knowledge development. But historically, people of color, living in conditions of turmoil, still held much stronger and more intellectually invigorating learning goals for their educational achievement. Given the richness in technology and resources that we have now, why can't we align to these same goals today? This shouldn't be an either/or challenge (Tatum, 2006), suggesting that we either have to advance students' identity and criticality or their content skills, knowledge, test preparation, and college readiness (see Figure below). Historically, our ancestors of color didn't make this distinction, so why do we have to choose one or the other now?

Historically, people of color, living in conditions of turmoil, still held much stronger and more intellectually invigorating learning goals for their educational achievement.

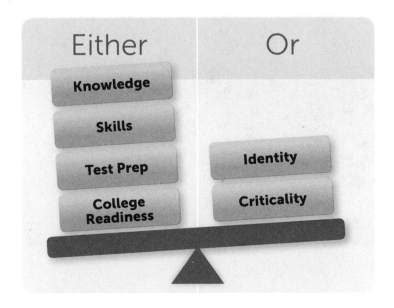

For this reason, over the past few years, I have been rewriting the Common Core State Standards and other state learning goals to infuse them with the Historically Responsive Literacy learning standards. The HRL Framework encourages educators to go beyond skills and knowledge in their lesson planning and practice. These goals build upon one another. If students know themselves, they are engaged with the confidence to learn the skills. If they have the skills, they can learn new knowledge and critique that knowledge. HRL as a theory teaches the whole child and is a framework for scaffolding learning that was designed for people of color and all underserved students. We must stop implementing curriculum and literacy models that were not designed for or by people of color, expecting that these models will advance the educational achievement of children of color. This is the same as designing a size 2 ball gown for a size 10 model. We expect youth to work inside frameworks that were not designed for them.

When we further consider these four pursuits (each discussed in upcoming chapters), we know that we are cultivating children's quality of life in their post K–12 experiences. When I think of the greatest leaders of our time, they hold identity (or a strong sense of self and others), plus skills, intellect, and criticality. On the other hand, the greatest oppressors of the world lack criticality and knowledge of self and of others. The next chapters will explicitly discuss each of the four pursuits of the HRL Framework.

Questions for Further Consideration: Teachers and Preservice Teachers

1. What are the histories of the students in your class? Think about their histories in the school, community, home, and wider society.

2. How do the students' histories connect to your content areas? How have their people historically contributed to the development of mathematics, science, social studies, literature, and language?

3. Who are your students? Whom do they say they are? Who do others say they are (think also how they are portrayed in the media)? Whom do they desire to be?

4. What are your students' literacy practices outside of the classroom? What do they read and write? How do they speak? What are the ways in which they know about the world around them?

5. How do the students' histories, identities, and literacies compare to your own?

Questions for Further Consideration: Principals and School Leaders

1. How do your interview questions screen potential teachers for culturally and historically responsive education? You may need to rewrite or revise interview questions to screen for teachers who are prepared to teach to respond to the students' identities and sociopolitical consciousness.

2. How does the diversity of teachers align with diversity of students and of the community?

3. Do students have teachers who look like them and share cultural identities? What are some ways you recruit teachers of color?

4. Are teachers prepared to teach in response to students' histories, identities, literacies, and language? How do you know?

5. Are you asking teachers to teach in culturally and historically responsive ways but implicitly pushing the teaching of skills or test preparation only? How do your observational and evaluation tools support the teaching of culturally and historically responsiveness?

Teaching and Learning With the Four-Layered HRL Framework

Part Two of this book focuses on each of the layers of the Historically Responsive Literacy Framework for Teaching and Learning. These include (1) identity development, (2) skills development, (3) intellectual development, and (4) criticality. These four learning goals are collectively called the Historically Responsive Literacy Framework. This Historically Responsive Literacy model was derived from examining historical artifacts related to the activities and philosophies of 19th-century Black literary societies. These layers were the four ways literacy was defined and education was advanced. In Chapters 3 to 6, each of the four learning goals is defined and explained with examples of instructional approaches. When these four learning pursuits are taught together, the learning becomes humanizing and more complete—giving students opportunities for personal, intellectual, and academic success. As educators strive to be responsive to the cultural and racial identities of our students and our times, learning standards must be recast to be more inclusive of intellectualism, identity, and criticality so these new frameworks actually improve education for all students and become a gauge to measure the quality of pedagogy.

Toward the Pursuit of Identity

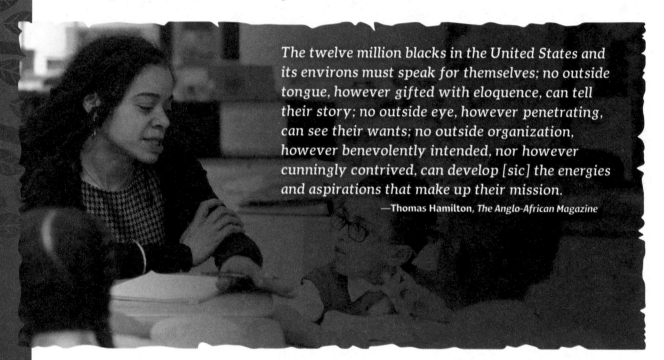

> The twelve million blacks in the United States and its environs must speak for themselves; no outside tongue, however gifted with eloquence, can tell their story; no outside eye, however penetrating, can see their wants; no outside organization, however benevolently intended, nor however cunningly contrived, can develop [sic] the energies and aspirations that make up their mission.
>
> —Thomas Hamilton, *The Anglo-African Magazine*

Identity matters. Identity was one of the first things to be stripped from enslaved Africans, thus it became key for people of color to know themselves so they could tell their own stories. Consequently, identity was also one of the first areas we sought to reclaim. In literacy learning, as early Black Americans were reading, writing, and speaking, they were learning about themselves and the lives of others. Literacy was integral to identity development and was not seen as an isolated effort in education. The editor of the *The Anglo-African Magazine* wrote the above in January 1859. His language speaks volumes to the necessity of Black people at the time (and arguably, today) to be seen and have their voices and stories honored. And although they may have had allies who supported their mission, even their allies could not have fully understood their experiences nor have been able to speak on their behalf. Historically, as Black people within 1800s literary societies read, wrote, and spoke about critical issues, they were also making sense of their collective African American identities and their individual identities. In fact, it was so enmeshed within their literacy practices that identity was defined as literacy in the larger conceptualization. The 1859 primary source document excerpted here also speaks to the importance of who gets to speak for people of color, particularly young people of color. Even teachers with the best intentions and practices are not the best people to speak for any student—the students must speak for themselves.

Cultivating Identity

When I work with teachers who struggle with teaching culturally and linguistically diverse youth, I often ask them to tell me about their students. Sadly, I am usually flooded with negative responses and comments about perceived weaknesses of the students in their schools and classrooms. In response to my question, I first hear things like, "my students don't like to read or write; my students can't read; my students aren't invested in their learning; my students' test scores are low; my students are unmotivated." I have many reactions and tensions around such comments. For one, I have never met an unmotivated child in my years working with youth. I have, however, "met" unmotivating curriculum and instruction.

Secondly, I unpack the use of the phrase "my students" and why teachers felt the students in their classrooms somehow *belonged* to them when they talk about them with such disparaging comments. I wonder if they would introduce their own children to strangers in similar ways. If not, why are we still "othering" children? This very problem prompted Lisa Delpit (2006) to write her book *Other People's Children: Cultural Conflict in the Classroom*. She writes about how some educators do not teach diverse students as their own and

Literacy was integral to identity development and was not seen as an isolated effort in education.

how the notion of "othering" marginalizes them. This practice is in direct conflict with cultural and historic responsiveness. I also recently had teachers tell me that after they got tenure, they had the choice to go back to teaching in very rote, unresponsive ways because they had more job security. I pushed back on this comment, because for Black educators and others who see children of color as their own people, they don't see "going back" to mediocrity as a choice, because it will be a failure for our people. We don't separate the progress of Black children, as an example, from the progress of our own people.

If we flip this notion of "other" further, we are actually teaching "other people's curriculum" in schools, because current curriculum

and standards are not typically written with our students' identities in mind, especially Black and Brown children. Most sanctioned curriculum is not our own. Curriculum today (including the Common Core State Standards) is not able to address meaning-making shaped by student identity. Moreover, the curricula, books, and mandated frameworks used across the nation are not usually designed for Black and Brown children, and these are the youth populations who have been underserved by education the most. These educational mandates are not normally written by educators and researchers of color. If we seek to get it right with populations that have been underserved by schools the most, a productive starting point must be to put sanctioned curricula in place designed by people of color for youth of color so that all educators and all children can achieve. If we seek to advance the educational development of youth, we must create frameworks that are written in response to their histories and identities.

When I asked teachers to tell me about the students in their schools and classrooms, I began to notice where they started students' stories. Some teachers' comments did not always reflect excellence and brilliance. Now, there are always the exceptions—teachers who rave about how wonderful, talented, and bright their students are. But we must challenge those teachers who judge their students from a deficit perspective. I asked teachers to close their eyes and think of their own shortcomings or faults. I asked them to consider that one thing they may have done in their past that they want to forget about—the thing that they hope to keep hidden due to embarrassment. I asked if they wanted someone else to introduce them to a group of strangers in this same way. They typically replied no. This all relates to where we begin our students' stories and who they are. We must start their stories and identities with their excellence.

What Is Identity?

Identity is composed of notions of who we are, who others say we are (in both positive and negative ways), and whom we desire to be. I believe there is a complex and dynamic dance among the three toward identity development for both children and adults throughout our lives. Identity is dynamic and changing. Our identities (both cultural identities and others) are continually being (re)defined and revised while we reconsider who we are within our sociocultural and sociopolitical environment. Identity is fluid, multilayered, and relational, and is also shaped by the social and cultural environment as well as by literacy practices (Sutherland, 2005). Examples may include racial, ethnic, cultural, gender, kinship, academic/intellectual, environmental, personal/individual, sexual, and community identities. Youth need opportunities in school to explore multiple facets of selfhood, but also to learn about the identities of others who may differ. If they are going to enjoy a quality of life and live alongside other people, they must deeply know themselves and the histories and truths of other diverse people. Knowing about the cultures of other people teaches them how to respect, love, and live in harmony with others who don't look or know the world as they do. Students should not have to wait until college or adulthood to discover self for the first time. They need spaces in K–12 classrooms to make sense of who they are and who they are not, because

We must start their stories and identities with their excellence.

students of color are flooded with images and representations in media, literature, and social media that depict their identities in deficit ways. In a 2010 summer literacy institute I facilitated for Black girls, one 16-year-old teenager wrote the following:

> *I have so many issues with it [identity] and I feel like no one really understands or at least not anyone I have encountered so it makes me self-conscious and I don't like to talk about it and sometimes I cry about it because not knowing who you are is the worst feeling in the world.*

This young person wrote something that reaffirmed the deep connections between identity and learning. The student was academically successful in high school, usually making high marks on classroom and national assessments. This child was performing well at a top-ranked high school and was positioned to get accepted into several strong colleges. During the first day, she wrote this in her journal, stating the discomfort with her personal sense of self and the great struggle with self-identity, which often made her cry. At a research meeting, I spoke publicly about this student and the importance of learning as a tool to shape identity. After this talk, a researcher commented that because the student had strong grades and could easily get accepted into prestigious universities, educators did not have to worry about students like her and should instead focus on students who "actually struggle." But what this person failed to honor was the child's voice and sense of self and the reality that for a Black/Latinx non-gender-conforming young person, academic learning was not enough to define success. This child needed more than grades or skills. She also needed to feel confident in knowing self.

For educators, it is critically important to push back on standards and practices that are not aligned to what students need most.

This conversation reaffirmed the importance of identity and learning goals and how the two cannot be separated and isolated. It also helped me to expand the purpose and power of instruction. Our goal is not just to help students become better test takers or academic achievers, but also for them to gain the confidence to use learning as a personal and sociopolitical tool to thrive in this world and to help them know themselves. This is why identity development is the first of the four pursuits in the HRL Framework. For educators, it is critically important to push back on standards and practices that are not aligned to what students need most. Researchers, especially, must work toward rectifying the thinking of others who claim identity doesn't matter (or matters less, compared to skills) in achievement with youth. Instead, a great deal of research has found that students have the potential for success when they see themselves in the curriculum and when their cultural, gender, and racial identities are affirmed (Noguera, 2003). Research on identity spans different fields in the social sciences. In the field of literacy education, identity has been honored and valued as an important aspect of literacy development by sociocultural and critical scholars. On the other hand, those who have solely privileged cognitive or traditional literacies alone have not emphasized or conceptualized identity with literacy development.

Students Must See Themselves in Their Learning

Our students, and arguably adults, are always looking for themselves in spaces and places. Before getting to literacy skill development such as decoding, fluency, comprehension, writing, or any other content-learning standards, students must authentically see themselves in the learning. When I work with teachers, I often take multiple pictures of them in small groups and project them on a large screen. Their eyes invariably go directly to their own faces. They look to find themselves. I believe students do the same in classrooms. They are looking for themselves. They are seeking to find curriculum and instructional practices that honor the multiple aspects of who they are. Who we are is connected to historical, institutional, political, and sociocultural factors. Consider leading thinker Ella Baker and the multiple layers of her identities. She was an activist, community organizer, daughter, journalist, director, planner, strategist, theorist, abolitionist, writer, and renowned, trusted public intellectual during the 20th century. When being responsive to students' identities, historically responsive practitioners ask, *How would I teach a young Ella Baker in my class given her identities? How would my instruction honor her psyche?* These questions are key because it is our job as educators to not just teach skills, but also to teach students to know, validate, and celebrate who they are.

Before getting to literacy skill development such as decoding, fluency, comprehension, writing, or any other content-learning standards, students must authentically see themselves in the learning.

As an example from my own life, I didn't truly understand my identities as a Muslim or Black girl until I was in college. I remember telling other children in my fifth-grade class about my imaginary Christmas gifts, which I didn't really have, because I was too afraid to not fit into the mainstream culture. My teachers also did not find any space to teach about Islam or my Muslim identity; nor did we read text written by Black women authors. This is a challenge because our identities and a strong sense of self are a form of protection and refuge for our children. If they don't know themselves, others will tell them who they are, in ways that may not be positive or accurate.

It's also our responsibility to cultivate the identities that are mostly connected to students' desired selves. Educators must learn about our students' future selves. I had a sixth-grade student who told me she was an activist because she engaged in action-oriented things to make her school community better. As her teacher, it was up to me to continue to cultivate and nurture this activist identity within her, even if she could not quite fully articulate her activism yet. I had to consider how an activism identity could be cultivated as I taught literature, English language arts, and social studies. The universal question is, *How will my instruction help students to learn something about themselves and/or about others?* To be responsive, we have to know students deeply. For example, if a Black boy explained that he's not a reader, I would help him connect to his lineage and heritage as a Black male. I would tell him that he came from generations of readers and thinkers and that reading is in his blood. In fact, African American literary societies were first developed by young Black males in 1828. This is a narrative about Black boys and men that is rarely told in the public media. Teachers should seek to help youth understand their identities because it helps them to see their own positionality and stances in the world and across sociopolitical issues. As students grow older, they experience angst trying to understand the world and their own personal beliefs and values. Young people are figuring out how to exist in the world apart from their parents. Classroom instruction should provide an avenue to explore the world and self.

Ways to Understand and Teach Identity

Here are some suggestions for helping teachers learn and understand the identities of their students.

Ask Students How They See Themselves

Ask students to tell you in their own words how they see their various identities. And when they tell you who they are, listen and trust them. As illuminated in the primary source document that opened this chapter, our students are the best people to speak about their own lives. Our young people of color have a history of others speaking for them or telling their stories without their permission. They also have a history of perpetuated images in the media that still continue today. Take, for example, the Cook's Soap Company, which put out racist ads in the early 1900s to express that their soap would make people whiter, cleaner, and better. One ad shows a Black boy using their soap and smiling because he becomes white; beneath the image, the caption reads, "Cook's Soap Turns Black White." Fast forward to today—we can look at a recent advertisement of a dark girl taking off her dark-colored T-shirt and then suddenly becoming a White girl, wearing a white T-shirt after using soap. When young people internalize these images, they may begin to feel their dark skin isn't beautiful or good enough.

A vintage color postcard advertising Cook's Lightning Soap published in Great Britain, circa 1905. (Photo by Paul Popper/Popperfoto/Getty Images)

There are many ways teachers can ask students who they are. They could engage in conversations with them directly, or have them read text related to who they are. They could also have them write about their lives and through writing, critique the deficit ways others have portrayed those who share similar identities. Some questions teachers could ask include:

- Who are you? Do you know who you are?
- What's your name? What does it mean?
- What are your cultural identities? (Think about how cultural identities typically have beliefs, languages that are used, literature read and written, power structure/social organization, rites of passages, rituals, traditions, celebrations, practices and a history.)
- How would you describe yourself to someone who didn't know you?
- What would your other teachers say about you?
- What would your family say about you?
- What would your friends say about you?
- What do you read, write, or think about in your home and community?
- How are people like you depicted in society and in the media?
- How might you describe your culture or ethnicity?
- How is science, math, social studies, or English language arts important in your culture/ethnicity?
- Do you feel that my teaching reflects your culture? If yes, how? If not, how could it be improved?
- If you could take me somewhere to help me understand your culture/ethnicity, where would you take me?

Engaging in dialogue or writing will help youth to know that they have a powerful voice and will help them to know, too, that their perspectives are being valued. There have been too many data meetings, curriculum meetings, or problem-solving meetings without students' voices at the table. Adults think that reading the research and listening to one another is enough. And while these are great sources of information, there is nothing better than hearing from the students themselves. To extend this exercise, the teacher could also interview parents and family members and invite them in co-constructing the curriculum.

Do a Brief "Who Are You?" Exercise

During my work with teachers, I often have them pair up, decide who is "a" and "b," and then take one-minute turns asking each other the question "Who are you?" They ask this repeatedly, and each time, the other person must answer differently. When teachers practice this exercise, I think they find it surprisingly difficult to continue to answer this question for 60 seconds. They usually start by responding with the observable qualities of what others see, and as the seconds go on, they respond with deeper unobservable qualities and identities of their lives. They also report that depending on how comfortable and safe they feel with the other person, they are willing to "unmask" and share more about themselves. And how people ask "Who are you?" usually denotes the type of answer they will get. When children engage in this exercise with one another, they usually start with their names. They may answer in adjectives or the ways others see them. I ask teachers to try to have students engage in this exercise regularly from the beginning to end of the school year. If they struggle with it, they can write or web the aspects of their identities.

Tell Our Name Stories

It is through our names that we first place ourselves in the world. Our names, being the gift of others, must be made our own...They must become our masks and our shields and the containers of all those values and traditions which we learn and/or imagine as being the meaning of our familial past.

—from *Hidden Name and Complex Fate* by Ralph Ellison

A slave should have no sense of himself that was separate from the self the master wanted him to have. Thus it was that no black had a name of his own. He was given the surname of his owner, no matter how many owners he might have during his life. A Negro has got no name. My father was a Ransom and he had a uncle named Hankin. If you belong to Mr. Jones and he sell you to Mr. Johnson, consequently you go by the name of your owner. Now where you get a name? We are wearing the name of our master. I was first a Hale; then my father was sold and then I was named Reed. Without a name of his own, the slave's ability to see himself apart from his owner was lessened. He was never asked who he was.

—from *To Be a Slave* by Julius Lester

On the first day of school, my teacher, Miss Mdingane, gave each of us an English name and said that thenceforth that was the name we would answer to in school. This was the custom among Africans in those days and was undoubtedly due to the British bias of our education.

—from *Long Walk to Freedom* by Nelson Mandela

If I'm gonna tell a real story, I'm gonna start with my name.

—Kendrick Lamar

Oftentimes, the first day of school can be brutal for culturally diverse children with names that don't fit in the mainstream culture. One way a teacher told me that names don't fit in the mainstream culture is when you can't find your name on a key chain at the pharmacy store. As Gholnecsar Muhammad, I always knew that the teacher had come to my name when reading the class roster during the first day, because she would take a long pause. The teacher would then move to making sounds that showed her discomfort with trying to pronounce my name.

Following this, she quickly went to, "Do you have a nickname?" This not only dismissed my name but my identity.

Names are not just names. It is typically through our names that we are first introduced to the world. And as Ralph Ellison pointed out, our names are a gift from others and must be made our own. Our names carry our cultures, values, traditions, and past. Different cultures have unique naming traditions. In Islamic culture, when a woman gets married, she typically keeps her last name, and when a child is adopted, the new family cannot change the child's previous name. There are cultures where the child takes the last name of both parents. In others, the social context of the time influences a child's name. Due to cultural practices, children are named after someone significant, and names also carry significant meaning. When I invite students to discuss or write name stories, I ask who named them, what their name means, what they know about their family's cultural naming practices—and then I ask them to describe one of their own name stories. This leads to asking critical questions about names and society. This particular list of questions was taken from *Facing History and Ourselves* (2015).

- What do our names reveal about our identities? What do they hide?
- What is the relationship between our names and our cultural identities?
- What do names suggest about the degree of freedom we have in society? Are some "names" treated differently than others?
- To what extent do we choose the names and labels others use for us?
- What parts of our identities do we choose for ourselves?
- What parts are chosen for us by others or by society? (p. 2)

What I appreciate about these questions is that they get to the power and equity that is embedded in our names. I am reminded of the countless studies that show that people with ethnic names typically experience discrimination such as not being called for an interview. This has led to many people of color feeling the need to shorten their names, give nicknames to ease pronunciation challenges, or even changing their names to fit in with Whiteness. When students write and tell their name stories, they, along with teachers, begin to learn more about who they are. To extend this, students can write personal narratives or autobiographies.

Selected Name Texts for Student Learning

- *I Know Why the Caged Bird Sings* by Maya Angelou
- *The Name Jar* by Yangsook Choi
- *The House on Mango Street* by Sandra Cisneros
- *To Be a Slave* by Julius Lester
- *Long Walk to Freedom* by Nelson Mandela
- *Alma and How She Got Her Name* by Juana Martinez-Neal
- *My Name Is Yoon* by Helen Recorvits
- *My Name Is Sangoel* by Karen Williams, Khadra Mohammed

Create Digital Stories

Students are encouraged to use multimodal technology (photographs, video, animation, sound, performance, print, etc.) to capture the dynamics of their lives and identities. Students are asked to digitally capture aspects of their communities and lives to tell a story of who they are. They may tell a story of their neighborhoods, communities, families, or any other context or cultural membership that shapes their lives and literacy practices. They then creatively put the story together in a visual presentation. This can be created for just the student or presented to the entire class.

Engage Deeply in Black Studies

Studying the histories of Black communities, given the wide and varied ways of what it means to be Black, is a good starting place for learning about racially, culturally, and linguistically diverse students. Focusing on Black studies (also Africana studies or African diaspora studies) is a study of the world that positions teachers in a space to learn about the history of oppression. Whatever histories and countries are searched, you will find examples of the marginalization of people of color. Black studies is a very intersectional discipline that examines wide variables of history, culture, institutionalized racism, and sociopolitical contexts.

If Black studies is understood, the hope is that the teacher becomes better prepared to respond to the needs of students of color and other marginalized students in schools. This becomes a precursor for understanding the cause for culturally responsive education. It will also help to explain the current context of schools and student achievement. If teachers have Black and Brown students in their classrooms, it is a necessity to study the histories and scholarship of their students' people. The intersectionality that is held in Black studies programs should serve to guide educators  on questions we should ask and ways we should approach curriculum and instruction. Studies in this area will push teachers to reframe traditional questions.

From—*What did the student do?*
To—*What was done to the student?*

From—*Why is the student struggling?*
To—*Why are the curricula, systems, and institutions struggling?*

From—*What are the results of the state achievement test?*
To—*What other outcomes can I measure that are just as meaningful?*

From—*Why can't the student read?*
To—*Where should I start students' stories and histories?*

Teaching Identities as a Learning Pursuit

It is important to note that before educators begin to teach students to know themselves and others, teachers must first do their own self-work. This work involves teachers deeply unpacking their own histories, identities, biases, assumptions, and tensions with racism and other oppressions they have learned, experienced, and practiced. I ask teachers to be honest about who they are and who they are not. In other words, if they have no intention of teaching young children to know and celebrate their lives, they need to begin that work with themselves. Or if they have good intentions but then fail to push toward action, that's also problematic. I ask teachers if they are armchair revolutionaries who profess their support for change but only look at it comfortably from their chairs. We need teachers who are on the front lines modeling, guiding students, participating, and doing what we ask of students. Teachers must ask if they will be transformed by the learning as they expect and want students to be transformed. Teachers cannot get to skills or content-learning standards until students see and know themselves in the curriculum designed for them.

The next step is to ask, "How will this lesson/unit plan help my students to learn something about themselves or others?" This question calls for teachers to think creatively about their design for teaching and learning. Rather than thinking of themselves solely as teachers, they need to think of themselves as designers of curriculum and instruction. After the content, topic, or text is selected, teachers must think about how it connects to students' lives and how it can be an opportunity to advance their knowledge of self or others. For example, take the text, "What Is Your Life's Blueprint?" This was a talk Dr. Martin Luther King Jr. gave to a group of junior high students. In the text, he says:

> I want to ask you a question, and that is: What is your life's blueprint? Whenever a building is constructed, you usually have an architect who draws a blueprint, and that blueprint serves as the pattern, as the guide, and a building is not well erected without a good, solid blueprint.

Now each of you is in the process of building the structure of your lives, and the question is whether you have a proper, a solid and a sound blueprint…

The concept of a blueprint is a fascinating topic to explore across content areas. If English teachers were teaching this text, they may focus on writing personal narratives. Science teachers could focus on the blueprint of DNA. Math teachers could teach about measurement and scale, and social studies teachers could focus on the history of America's blueprint and who built this country. As teachers are teaching their content-area skills, they are also connecting the topic to the students in their classrooms and their identities. In this sample Historically Responsive Literacy learning plan, students will think about their own goals or blueprints in their lives.

Lesson Sample

Identity: Students will learn about their own blueprints in life. (*personal identity*)

Skills:

- **English/Language Arts:** Students will produce clear and coherent writing (personal narratives) in which the development, organization, and style are appropriate to task, purpose, and audience.
- **Science:** Students will understand the pattern of inheritance, analyze Punnett squares, and statistically analyze data results on inheritance.
- **Math:** Students will examine measurement and scale for designing blueprints.
- **Social Studies:** Students will examine the history of America's blueprint and who built this country.

Intellect: Students will learn about architecture and blueprints.

Criticality: Students will learn the barriers that inhibit people from overcoming adversity and reaching their life's goals.

Knowing self prepares young people to live joyfully in the world—a world that may tell them negative things about who they are. This is why young people need to know themselves as well as others who may be different from them. This knowledge will help prevent them from oppressing people who are different from them in the future. It also teaches young people how to love and live with differences as they grow older.

Questions for Further Consideration: Teachers and Preservice Teachers

1. Who am I?
2. Which ideologies and social conditioning have shaped my knowledge and perspectives of people of Black and Brown children?
3. How can my instruction authentically respond to my students' identities?
4. How do I focus on the beauty and brilliance of children in my class?
5. How will each lesson or unit plan help students to know something about their identities or the identities of others?

Questions for Further Consideration: Principals and School Leaders

1. Who am I?
2. How does my leadership style(s) connect to my own identities?
3. Which ideologies and social conditioning have shaped my knowledge and perspectives of people of Black and Brown children?
4. How are students and their families' identities honored and validated in my leadership?
5. What do I know (and still need to learn) about the histories of the students and their families? Do my meetings and programs connect to this knowledge?

Toward the Pursuit of Skills

During his recent sojourn in Philadelphia...the Editor of The Liberator had the privilege of visiting and addressing a society of colored ladies called the 'FEMALE LITERARY ASSOCIATION.' It was one of the most interesting spectacles he had ever witnessed. If the traducers of the colored race could be acquainted with the moral worth, just refinement, and large intelligence of this association, their mouths would hereafter be dumb. The members assemble together every Tuesday evening, for the purpose of mutual improvement in moral and literary pursuits. Nearly all of them write, almost weekly, original pieces, which are put anonymously into a box, and afterward criticised by a committee... This society is...composed of about twenty members, but is increasing, and full of intellectual promise.

—William Garrison, *The Liberator*, 1831

This column from 1831 is prefaced with a kneeling woman with the words, "Am I not a Woman and a Sister?" The image depicts an appeal for social justice and change and was a mission for the women of the Female Literary Association (see facing page).

Following the captioned image were written details of the literacy enactments described from William Garrison, who we know was the editor of *The Liberator*. He visited one of the society's weekly meetings and described the members as having "moral worth, just refinement, and large intelligence." He explained that they met on Tuesday evenings to engage in literary pursuits—including the cultivation of skills.

Cultivating Skills

One of the literary pursuits Garrison described is the process of critiquing and revising drafts of writing. He explained that the young women's writings were placed in a box and then selected and critiqued by other members. Sharing and shaping their writings through this peer critique created stronger compositions—and exemplifies the skill development that took place in the literary societies. Historically, writing was the ultimate intellectual and literary skill because it entailed the act of reading something, thinking about the content, considering new ideas to set to paper, and then communicating those words to the intended audience. After something was written, it was usually discussed, debated, and used to address the public. In this chapter, I focus on the skill of writing development because it should be cultivated in each content area as it was historically. It is, however, important to note that many skills across disciplines were cultivated in and around these literary spaces.

Members of literary societies cultivated skills and wrote across a variety of genres, including speeches, essays, personal narratives, letters, news (domestic and foreign), journal articles, announcements of marriages and deaths, and minutes from societies and other organizations. Their literary writings included poetry, short stories, and lengthier works.

LADIES' DEPARTMENT.

'Am I not a Woman and a Sister?'

White Lady, happy, proud and free,
Lend awhile thine ear to me;
Let the Negro Mother's wail
Turn thy pale cheek still more pale.
Can the Negro Mother joy
Over this her captive boy,
Which in bondage and in tears,
For a life of wo she rears?
Though she bears a Mother's name,
A Mother's rights she may not claim;
For the white man's will can part,
Her darling from her bursting heart.

From the Genius of Universal Emancipation.
LETTERS ON SLAVERY.—No. III.

The members also worked toward improving their reading skills and read a wealth of literature, which enabled their writings. Members did not limit their reading and writing to one particular genre, author, or form of text. Instead, they read from a variety of outlets on diverse subjects and authorship, as noted in the September 11, 1841 issue of *The Colored American* in which the author writes about "useful literature" for the education of people of color. The author introduces a monthly periodical to be read and written by African American people.

> It is devoted, to Literature, Science, and the Arts, including Useful Knowledge, American Biography, Scenery, National Historical, Essays, Poetry, Specimens of Eloquence, Accounts of Eminent Artists, Sketches of Society and Customs, Reviews, Travels, and Miscellaneous Literature. If the able pens to be enlisted in this work shall essay upon the various subjects here promised, it can but be not only an interesting, but a very useful working in extending English literature.

This writer details the diverse nature of their texts. Just as importantly, it is essential for today's youth to read, write, and think about diverse sets of literature in multimodal forms in order to develop their literacy skills. In turn, with these skills, they have more access to the content knowledge in math, science, literature, and social studies. Historically, skills were cultivated because skills across areas of learning gave students, young and old alike, the access and tools for education. They learned and mastered the important skills for English and language, mathematics, history, and the sciences. Literacy skills were grounded in student learning and engagement across the disciplines. In one example detailing their activities, it was written:

Historically, skills were cultivated because skills across areas of learning gave students, young and old alike, the access and tools for education.

> A flourishing literary society is maintained in this district, with meetings twice per week—one for discussions, and the other for the reading of original compositions, declamations, and other literary exercises.

This was published in *The Liberator* and speaks to the importance of literacy skills. This is why it is key for literacy to be cultivated across the academic disciplines. In other words, literacy skills should not be taught or exercised only in literature or English language arts classes but in all spaces of learning, including health, physical education, art, and music.

What Are Skills?

Skills and proficiencies are often measured using quantitative, high-stakes assessments. I use *skills* and *proficiencies* interchangeably to denote competence, ability, and expertise based on what educators deem to be important for student learning in each content area. Skills are central to the ways in which we do school today and typically define achievement standards. Skills are also significant in designing learning standards that govern teaching and learning in schools, and each content area has its own descriptions and set of skills. I often ask who gets to set the pacing guides, curriculum, state assessments, and learning standards. When I ask teachers who the decision-makers are behind these efforts, they typically don't know, nor do they know who is designing the plan of action for American schools. This is problematic because it is the skills outlined in state standards, state tests, and evaluation frameworks that govern the curriculum and instruction for schools. So, who develops them? Are they people of color? Are they teachers who embody a sociopolitical consciousness? Do they deeply know the history of race and equity in this country?

> *I use skills and proficiencies interchangeably to denote competence, ability, and expertise based on what educators deem to be important for student learning in each content area.*

Skills embody the learning standards that are promoted by states. Standards-based education started more formally after the publication of *A Nation at Risk* in 1983. This report, given by President Ronald Reagan's National Commission on Excellence in Education, presented a landscape of skill proficiencies of Americans. In the report, authors speak of the importance of competition and "educational performance," which is compared to an act of war:

> Our Nation is at risk. Our once unchallenged preeminence in commerce, industry, science, and technological innovation is being overtaken by competitors throughout the world.... If an unfriendly foreign power had attempted to impose on America the mediocre

educational performance that exists today, we might well have viewed it as an act of war.

The authors of this report documented some examples of the landscape of educational performance and included statements such as:

- Some 23 million American adults are functionally illiterate by the simplest tests of everyday reading, writing, and comprehension.

- About 13 percent of all 17-year-olds in the United States can be considered functionally illiterate. Functional illiteracy among minority youth may run as high as 40 percent.

- Average achievement of high school students on most standardized tests is now lower than 26 years ago when Sputnik was launched.

- Many 17-year-olds do not possess the "higher-order" intellectual skills we should expect of them. Nearly 40 percent cannot draw inferences from written material; only one-fifth can write a persuasive essay; and only one-third can solve a mathematics problem requiring several steps.

- Business and military leaders complain that they are required to spend millions of dollars on costly remedial education and training programs in such basic skills as reading, writing, spelling, and computation. The Department of the Navy, for example, reported to the Commission that one-quarter of its recent recruits cannot read at the ninth-grade level, the minimum needed simply to understand written safety instructions. Without remedial work, they cannot even begin, much less complete, the sophisticated training essential in much of the modern military.

When we look closely at just these points, we see there is a high focus on skills and not on other important qualities such as identity, anti-racism, and criticality. We wonder why these qualities are rarely mentioned in schools across the nation. Government leaders do not even mention these essential qualities in a report meant to provide an overview of the state of education in the United States. These goals are not at the forefront; rather, the skills and other selected elements that educators and policy makers think are easily measured become the focus. Literacy, too, is a focal point, and the report reveals that students did not score high on assessments of literacy. Or as another way of explaining it, systems, schools and instruction have not helped students achieve at their highest potential—and yet, these institutions and systems continue without critical examination or challenge.

This report also prompted more of the high-stakes testing that we see today, along with the over-reliance on the scores that result from these tests. These exams determine life outcomes and access into other academic and professional arenas for youth. The onus of low scores is placed on the students themselves instead of the media, government, schools, instruction, or systems, which all play a role in student achievement. For example, a report from a group of Black students who took the NAEP test in 2017 told us that (according to this one test) 20 percent of fourth-grade students are proficient in the area of reading. NAEP, of course, is a measurement of skills only and defines students at or above the Proficient Level as those who "demonstrate solid academic performance and competency over challenging subject matter" (2018). They also note that the Proficient Level "does not represent grade-level proficiency as determined by other assessment standards (e.g., state or district assessments)." If we look closer at this 20 percent proficiency of Black students in 2017, it says that the nation is really "at risk" for getting it right with 80 percent of Black children. This should spark outrage and alarm for all of humankind. In 1992 (almost 10 years after *A Nation at Risk*), we failed 92 percent of Black fourth-grade students. The percentages of eighth graders are not far off, as NAEP reported 9 percent (1992); 16 percent (2015); and 18 percent (2017) reading proficiency of Black students. Again, this is the population we have mostly failed as a nation. Our Black students are not failing; it is the systems, instruction, and standards created to monitor, control, and measure a very narrow definition of achievement that are off the mark. Most important, instruction is ahistorical for Black children.

> *Schools and instruction have not helped students achieve at their highest potential—and yet, these institutions and systems continue without critical examination or challenge.*

A Framework for Literacy

Across the nation, we continue to work toward an ideal of transformative literacies, yet we use frameworks, curricula, and instructional tools that were not expressly designed for our students of color, the population who have been underserved the most.

Let's consider a medical analogy. One could notice that the highest-ranked and most honored surgeons are the ones who can keep someone who is near death alive. These doctors not only use what they learned in books, but they also use their instinctive knowledge and creativity to heal. I am not comparing our children of color to patients in a hospital, but their literacy development is deeply connected to their lives and to their life outcomes. We need the highest-ranked teachers to help them thrive in this world in much the same way.

We cannot continue to design new frameworks that have traditionally only served the mainstream, or are designed to advance skills alone, and hope that they also help children of color. Hope alone is not enough. We need to

As they were reading the social context toward freedom, they were also acquiring the skills necessary for reading and understanding print.

be designers in curriculum, instruction, and leadership to get it right with those who need it the most. They depend on us. From 1983 to today, we have not seen academic acceleration or any major climbs in academic achievement for all children. More than 35 years later, what has changed or shifted? Why are we still clinging to the same approaches for our youth in schools? In the last 25 years, we have climbed only 8 percentage points across the nation in fourth-grade reading. Most of the students continue to fall within basic levels of reading. Historically, Black people in the 19th century were not basic. Nor did they have basic goals for education. Around the time of *A Nation at Risk* and onward, we heard terms like "at-risk youth," which has been used to label Black and Brown youth. Yet, what are they at risk of? Poor instruction? Racism? Instruction disconnected to their identities and histories? A skills-only curriculum? These are the questions we need to be asking today.

In our literacy classrooms, we often see a push for skills such as reading comprehension, fluency, vocabulary development, and writing mechanics. We know that these skills and others are essential for youth to achieve, and historically, Black readers and writers developed traditional literacy skills in the service of their elevated goals—intellectual and moral enrichment. They understood that literacy skills were a means to build greater conduits to liberation. If they could advance multiple forms of literacy skills, they could read, write, teach, and communicate with others to build capacity. As they were reading the social context toward freedom, they were also acquiring the skills necessary for reading and understanding print. Typically, when people think of the word *literacy*, their minds go directly to skills. Although we know literacy is much more than skills, it is also important that students develop the skills necessary for each content area.

Ways to Learn, Understand, and Teach Writing Skills

For teachers who want to help their students acquire the skills they need to write effectively, here are some suggested approaches.

Writing Autobiographies About Content

In graduate school when I was studying literacy, language, and culture, I had to write a position paper detailing my early experiences with reading, writing, and language. This became a narrative to help me understand how

my prior experiences impacted my current feelings about literacy education. This grounded my research and understanding of literacy development. It also helped my professor learn my past history with literacy, which informed his instruction. Similarly, I ask the teachers with whom I work to invite students to write their own biographies in math, science, language, and social studies—as a way to learn what experiences they had and need to have with content-area learning. Some students come to us without the same love and excitement we have for our discipline, perhaps because they failed to experience exciting and rich pedagogies in previous grades. This exercise also helps teachers to see where the writing skills of students are and what areas of writing development need more support. Some guiding questions teachers could ask include:

- What are your histories and past experiences with math, science, literature, or social studies?
- When did you fall in love with math, science, literature, or social studies?
- When did you begin to dislike math, science, literature, or social studies?

- What is the first time you had to practice or use math, science, literature, or social studies outside of school? Describe this experience.

- In which ways do you learn math, science, literature, or social studies best?

- How could math, science, literature, or social studies support your future goals in life?

The Urgency of Your Pen

When I was in graduate school, my mentor, Alfred Tatum, who taught me ways to make it impossible for students to fail, frequently asked, "What issues are most urgent of your pen?" This question calls on students to think about their identities and communities and determine those social issues that are most in need of change or improvement. When I ask this question of youth, they develop a list of issues that need more attention or revision. These issues then become the subject for learning within the different content areas. It becomes the charge of the teacher to intellectualize these topics and connect to other learning goals of skills development. In the past, students have written about issues such as:

- Love
- Police brutality
- Gentrification
- Lack of fairness or justice in news media
- Bullying and social media inflicting harm
- Air quality
- Clean water
- Cleanliness of neighborhoods
- Quality schools

Students then research their selected topics and begin to write, revise, and write more.

Teach the Language of Writing Assessment

When we engage students in writing, teachers need to write with their students and teach the assessment language of writing. Depending on the genre of writing, this assessment language may reflect different elements. When Dr. Tatum facilitated the African American Adolescent Male Summer Literacy Institute and I facilitated Black Girls WRITE (Writing to Represent our Identities, our Times, and our Excellence), I used the following rubrics and assessment language. Both of these contemporary literacy institutes reflected Black literary societies of the past. We taught and offered many examples (including my own writing) of these writing skill elements:

Poetry

Interest Level and Momentum	The piece is interesting and keeps the reader involved.
Authenticity	The piece seems genuine.
Details	The author provides vivid and necessary details.
Word Choice	The author chooses strong words that capture the reader's attention.
Style	The style of the prose speaks to the content, purpose, and audience.
Voice	The voice seems real and authentic.
Accurate and Aesthetic	This piece has factual and/or personal, emotional content.
Research and Knowledge	The writing draws evidence from informational texts, including multiple print and digital sources.

Literary/Narrative Writing

Organization	The events and ideas in the story follow a logical sequence.
Clarity and Coherence	The language is clear and comprehensible.
Interest Level and Momentum	The piece is interesting and keeps the reader engaged.
Setting	The piece is clearly situated in a time and place (setting); engages and orients the reader by establishing a context.
Authenticity	The piece seems real and believable.
Details	The author provides vivid and necessary descriptive details and sensory language to capture the action and convey experiences and events.
Word Choice	The author chooses strong words that capture the reader's attention.
Style	The style of the prose speaks to the content, purpose, and audience and is maintained throughout the writing. The author uses narrative techniques, such as dialogue, pacing, description, and reflection, to develop experiences, events, and/or characters.
Voice	The voice seems real and authentic.
Accurate and Aesthetic	This piece has factual and/or personal, emotional content.
Research and Knowledge	The writing draws evidence from informational texts, including multiple print and digital sources.
Transitions	The author uses a variety of transition words, phrases, and clauses to convey sequence, signal shifts from one time frame or setting to another, and show the relationships among experiences and events.
Conclusion	The author provides a conclusion that follows from and reflects on the narrated experiences or events.

Informational Writing

Introduction	The topic is introduced clearly and effectively previews what is to follow.
Organization	The events, concepts, ideas, and information follow a logical sequence.
Clarity and Coherence	The language is clear and comprehensible.
Interest Level and Momentum	The piece is interesting and keeps the reader engaged.
Details	The author provides vivid and necessary details.
Support	The author introduces claim(s) about a topic or issue, acknowledges and distinguishes the claim(s) from alternate or opposing claims, and organizes the reasons and evidence logically. There is a relationship among ideas. The information supports the topic(s).
Word Choice	The author chooses precise language and domain-specific vocabulary to inform about or explain the topic.
Style	The style of the prose speaks to the content, purpose, and audience and is maintained throughout the writing.
Accurate and Aesthetic	This piece has both factual and/or personal, emotional content.
Research and Knowledge	The writing draws evidence from informational texts, including multiple print and digital sources.
Transitions	The author uses appropriate and varied transitions to create cohesion and clarify the relationships among ideas and concepts.
Conclusion	The author provides a concluding statement or section that follows from and supports the information or explanation presented.

First, the teacher should teach the genre of the writing, whether students are writing responses to literature or a word problem or writing poetry or essays. This is best accomplished by using several examples of authentic and meaningful texts. Then it is important to craft elements and assessment language of that particular genre and connect them to the learning standards. Then students need to learn those elements and practice their writing with several stages of feedback from peers and the teacher.

Mentor Texts for Writing Development

Writing researchers have found that literary mentors provide excellent support for students across all aspects of writing development. The form of mentor texts has been expanded over time to include not only print material, but also multimodal texts of nontraditional media (i.e., magazines, blogs, flash fiction, popular culture texts, and slam poetry). Additionally, the role and purpose of mentor texts have been varied. While teachers have used mentor texts to introduce young writers to varied genres for young writers, teachers are also using mentor texts to help their students understand the structures of grammar and the mechanics of writing. Teachers should select mentor texts to support students' reading, writing, and thinking skills around the potential to cultivate students' skills, identities, intellect, and criticality.

Teach the Skills of Historians, Scientists, Mathematicians, and Writers

Teachers should ask themselves how historians, scientists, mathematicians, and writers read, write, and think. One of my mothers, who is a historian, always questions the source of everything she reads. So, this means if social studies teachers are engaging students in class, they should have students question everything that they read and hear. This also teaches the academic literacies of each content area. Some of these literacies include:

- *English Language Arts*: reading, writing, and speaking about the who, what, when, where, and why; the literal meaning versus implied meaning; themes of text; text structures; genres/types of text

- *Math*: search for truth and errors; importance of each word and symbol; interpretation of information; modeling and problem-solving

- *Science*: facts based on evidence; developing questions; graphics, charts; data analysis, hypothesis, observations, and investigation

- *History/Social Studies*: interrogating sources; author's perspective and bias; time period/contextualization; comparing multiple perspectives and documents; rhetorical constructions (Jetton & Shanahan, 2012)

Teachers can then engage students in an "expert panel" setting, where students sit on a panel and give summaries of skills and take questions from the rest of the class.

Teaching Skills as a Learning Pursuit

Teaching skills is important, but teaching them alone is highly problematic and also should not be privileged over other goals or pursuits discussed in this book. Instead, skills should be taught alongside other pursuits. This will call for teachers to be skillful in teaching but also skillful in the discipline they teach. They must be experts in their disciplines and see literature, language, mathematics, and science in different situations and aspects of life. Teachers must love their disciplines and be masterful in the skills they teach to students. Not being experts and lovers of the discipline could cause students to do poorly in the classroom.

Skills need to be cultivated for the enhancement of the mind. On the evening of June 12, 1828, William Whipper addressed the Colored Reading Society of Philadelphia for Mental Improvement. In his speech, he introduced the literary society and discussed the importance of the organization for skills and mental improvement. He also listed several key stipulations that governed the structure of the organization and the specific skills it would cultivate. In the fourth stipulation, he explained that all membership dues received would be spent on what he called "useful books," to be in the care of the Society's librarian. Later in the speech he explained one of the following skill goals for educational improvement:

"Close and accurate thinking, and to acquire a facility of classifying and arranging, analyzing and comparing our ideas on different subjects" could easily be language written in the Common Core State Standards or other learning standards.

> The first object of education is to exercise, and by exercising to improve the faculties of the mind. Every faculty we possess is improvable by exercise. This is a law of nature. The acquisition of knowledge is not the only design of a liberal education; its primary design is to discipline the mind itself, to strength and enlarge its powers, to form habits of close and accurate thinking, and to acquire a facility of classifying and arranging, analyzing and comparing our ideas on different subjects. Without this preparatory exercise, our ideas will be superficial and obscure, and all the knowledge we acquire will be but a confused mass thrown together without arrangement, and incapable of useful application.

The line detailing *close and accurate thinking, and to acquire a facility of classifying and arranging, analyzing and comparing our ideas on different subjects* could easily be language written in the Common Core State Standards or other learning standards. Whipper states that without skills, ideas and intellectualism would be "superficial and obscure." Our students need the skills to access the knowledge learned; otherwise, knowledge is a confused mass without useful application. We want students to act on the knowledge they learn. Therefore, teaching skills must also be regarded as a pursuit and not trapped in disengaging small or minor activities in the classroom and school.

Lesson Sample

Identity: Students will connect their identities as (future) travelers. (*traveling identity*)

Skills:

- **English/Language Arts:** Students will determine two or more central ideas in a text and analyze their development over the course of the text; provide an objective summary of the text.
- **Math:** Students will measure and calculate distance.
- **Science:** Students will examine vehicle emissions as a cause of air pollution.
- **Social Studies:** Students will investigate the history of travel and the construction and design of highways/interstates.

Intellect: Students will investigate the history of the Green Book.

Criticality: Students will identify ways African Americans experienced racial violence while traveling in the 1940s and 1950s.

Students need rich and meaningful experiences when learning skills—experiences that engage mind and heart and help shape positive school histories. We all have that one memorable experience from our own educational histories from that dynamic teacher we had. We want students to recall more than one experience.

Questions for Further Consideration: Teachers and Preservice Teachers

1. How does your mandated curriculum nurture and cultivate students' skills in your content area? Do you agree that these are the most important skills in your discipline area?

2. Do you perform and show the same skills you teach to students? For example, do you write essays and show your examples when you ask students to write essays?

3. What creative and innovative ways can you teach skills without lectures or worksheets?

4. What is one core experience you have for teaching skills in your content area—one that will leave a legacy for your teaching?

5. How can you teach beyond the learning standards offered in your district?

Questions for Further Consideration: Principals and School Leaders

1. What is the trend assessment data of your school? What has helped and not helped regarding the teaching of skills?

2. In your leadership, how much do you center test scores or skills instead of other learning goals?

3. How do you support teachers who struggle with the teaching of skills?

4. What programs or initiatives do you offer to help students or adults who struggle with learning or teaching skills?

5. Do you speak to the need of cultural responsiveness but only evaluate teachers on the teaching of skills? How can you reverse this?

Toward the Pursuit of Intellect

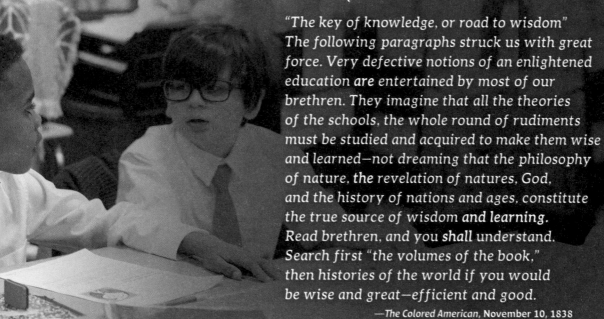

*"The key of knowledge, or road to wisdom" The following paragraphs struck us with great force. Very defective notions of an enlightened education are entertained by most of our brethren. They imagine that all the theories of the schools, the whole round of rudiments must be studied and acquired to make them wise and learned—not dreaming that the philosophy of nature, **the** revelation of natures, God, and the history of nations and ages, constitute the true source of wisdom **and learning.** Read brethren, and you **shall** understand. Search first "the volumes of the book," then histories of the world if you would be wise and great—efficient and good.*

—The Colored American, November 10, 1838

Across the world, there is a rich history of intellectualism. Readers in Black literary societies had aims of cultivating their intellect and scholarship so they could be better equipped to experience joy and to critique the problems of the world. In this excerpt, written and published in *The Colored American* on November 10, 1838, the writer discussed the importance of knowledge and the ways in which theories and knowledge in the world *must* be studied and acquired. Historically, African American people did not just want to accumulate knowledge to hold in their minds, but they sought to do something with the knowledge they gained— and put knowledge into action through their public addresses, writings, and learning, which were then passed on to future generations. The writer in this historical artifact expressed that people must study books and then histories of the world with the goal of being "wise and great." Reading the world dictated the topics they chose to read, write, speak, and learn about. And these topics were wide and varied and responded to critical issues affecting local and global communities.

When we compare this to problems of practice in schools, we find classroom curriculum typically goes unchanged for years rather than being dynamic and in a constant state of transition as a reaction to the events of the world, many of which affect the human condition. Also, there is not enough *historicizing* of knowledge across the content areas. To historicize means to connect a topic to history or to represent it as historical. I often suggest to teachers that they teach the history and meaning of their discipline during the first days of school rather than beginning with Chapter 1 of their textbooks, which may do little more than teach skills in isolation. As an example, teachers should teach students on the subject of "What does mathematics mean?" I asked this question once to a large group of high school math teachers, and no one knew, but they all saw the importance of learning the ways mathematics is defined. Mathematics (like all content areas or disciplines) has a rich history, and the ways it was conceptualized has changed over time. Teachers ought to teach the history of their disciplines—language arts, science, and social studies— as an intellectual endeavor. It also intellectualizes the content areas in which students will be engaged for the entire school year.

Readers in Black literary societies had aims of cultivating their intellect and scholarship so they could be better equipped to experience joy and to critique the problems of the world.

Cultivating Intellect

Historically, it was necessary to cultivate intellectualism because society and oppressors did not see Black people as useful, smart, or capable of rigorous learning. Of course, this deficit thinking is wrong and inhumane and still affects today's youth. To resist this way of thinking, Black people in literary societies throughout this time equipped their minds with intellect and the power of reasoning. They learned about topics that were not just important for their immediate context (the United States) but also the global world. Some of these include concepts related to politics, human rights and justice, economics, sociology, and business. As they read texts about these topics, they wrote about them and engaged in the intellectual pursuit of debating, which required them to learn multiple sides of an argument. Martin (2002) records examples of debates and the results within literary societies. Here are a few:

- April 15, 1858. "Has the course of Hon. Stephen A. Douglas on the Kansas-Nebraska question been consistent?" (This topic was discussed on several occasions. There is no indication how the members voted.)

- July 28, 1858. "In embracing religion, are men influenced by love [of] God or fear of punishment?" (Love won.)

- September 29, 1858. "Was the Noahian flood universal?" (It was not.) (p. 309)

Intellect and the pursuit to acquire it has historically been stripped from African Americans. Speaking to this, Henry Highland Garnet, who was a newspaper editor, pastor, and abolitionist, delivered a speech in 1843 to the National Negro Convention. In his address he stated:

> Nearly three million of your fellow citizens are prohibited by law and public opinion (which in this country is stronger than law) from reading the Book of Life. Your intellect has been destroyed as much as possible, and every ray of light they have attempted to shut out from your minds. The oppressors themselves have become involved in the ruin. They have become weak, sensual, and rapacious—they have cursed you—they have cursed themselves—they have cursed the earth which they have trod.

In this part of his address, Garnet speaks to the need to agitate systems that have prevented the learning and cultivation of intellect. He argues that the intellect of Black people has been destroyed, and he compares this intellect to "light." He suggests that when the light of a people is diminished, all of humankind is negatively affected. Knowing the oppressive history of the U.S. means that cultivating intellect also entails the importance of restoring what has been taken from our African American people—thereby benefiting all people. The following example, published in *The Colored American* on July 15, 1837, was written in a section entitled, "Things which concern Colored Americans":

> There is, perhaps, no other people in the world. So much interest in all the measures of moral and intellectual improvements, as the colored people of these United States. No other people have been so completely robbed, of all the rights of man, as have colored Americans. We have suffered bondage in the midst of freedom— we have been bourne down in poverty, and disgrace, whilst wealth and honors have abounded in our land. We have been kept in darkness and ignorance, while other classes of our fellow citizens have enjoyed light and learning, and liberty, unequalled in the history of nations. And now, I speak advisedly, the set time of our redemptions is come. How shall we think, and feel and act? We live not in an age of miracles, but in an age of faith and works.

In our day, effects result from causes—grand enterprises—great purposes are carried on, and accomplished by human agencies. If our colored population desire to be useful and respected—If they would have their rights and attain their level, they must use the means, and adopt the measures of elevation and respectability.

I find that intellectualism can be minimized in schools as the focus shifts to skills and test prep. Adding to the challenge is the emphasis on students' so-called "reading identity" or the guided reading level at which they read. Teachers may then find watered-down texts that speak to children's reading level and not to their full development or intellectual identities. Educators need to move beyond the teaching of skills alone and teach students new ideals in ways that enlarge their mental powers in the disciplines. They also need to recognize that guided reading is only one small part of the instructional day and that students need access to a wide range of intellectually invigorating text.

What Is Intellect and Intellectualism?

Intellect or knowledge is what we learn or understand about various topics, concepts, and paradigms. It is the understanding, enhancement, and exercising of mental powers and capacities that allow one to better understand and critique the world. Therefore, intelligence is connected to action. The HRL Framework starts with identity and skills because if these two pursuits are developed, the possibility is created for intellect, and when students develop intellectualism, they can express their ideas, work through justice-centered solutions to the world's problems, and expand their mental capacities. Some have connected the aims of intellectualism to higher-order or higher-level thinking, but historically among Black communities, intellectualism wasn't seen as exceptional learning—it was just the norm and the way they approached learning. Often, intellect becomes conflated with skills in the classroom. For example, when I ask my preservice teachers to tell me what goals they have for developing intellect, they list items such as decoding or fluency; these are skills. Intellect includes what we want students to become smarter about, but also creates a space for students to apply their learning in authentic ways connected to the world. Teachers must think about new concepts that they are teaching as they are addressing skills. This is why we must rethink the texts we place in front of students. Texts must be intellectually energizing enough to cultivate the genius inside of students.

Cultivating students' intellectualism means developing their mental culture—helping them plan their central aims for quality of life and showing them how to navigate society after high school. Therefore, intelligence isn't just about academics, but also emotional intelligence and self- and social awareness.

High-Stakes Tests and Deficit Views

There is a history of deficit ways of viewing intellect throughout history as well as a history of Black folks viewing their own intellectual excellence. The former was perpetuated by folks who sought to create inferiority among Black people. A century after Black people were organizing around literacy in the 1800s, psychologists were developing I.Q. tests to measure intelligence. These became a mechanism for tracking students, predicting their academic success, or marginalizing them. The test unfairly labeled students— especially students of color. This contributed to false narratives related to the achievement gap that often compared Black and White students. Today, schools still compare Black and Latinx students to White students even when White students aren't performing the highest on the state assessment. This shows that in their minds, White is always the standard. These so-called gaps in achievement do not account for the decades of dismissive control and educational oppression faced by Black people and others who have experienced disparities.

I.Q. tests influenced the development of academic standards and standardizing testing in schools, yet they were (and still remain) deeply incomplete and biased at assessing students and determining achievement. We know that these tests lack diversity of thought. Also, the life experiences and characters written into the story excerpts and question prompts are disconnected from many students' lives. Many of us can recall the episode on the *Good Times* TV series called "The I.Q. Test"

Some have connected the aims of intellectualism to higher-order or higher-level thinking, but historically among Black communities, intellectualism wasn't seen as exceptional learning—it was just the norm and the way they approached learning.

when the character of Michael Evans took the test at school. Michael left the test early without completing the exam, and his parents later sat with him to ask him why he walked out, as this seemed uncharacteristic for their son. Michael responds with, "Mama, they don't know it, but that I.Q. exam was nothing but a white racist test." His mom, Florida, asks how it could be a "white racist test," since children of all colors take the same test. Michael's retort was that the test was created, written, and scored by White people—implying that it was not designed for Black children or others who did not live common experiences of White America. "It doesn't tell you how smart you are, just how white you are," he says. Michael goes on to tell his parents that his experience with the I.Q. test explains the so-called gaps in achievement that exist in education. He explains that the test is culturally biased and gives an example of a test question: "Cup and...." Students have to finish the phrase and select from the following words, "wall, saucer, table, or window." He adds that his friend Eddie selected "cup and table, because in his house, they don't have no saucers to put under the cup."

The test creators assume that all children have certain items in their homes. His dad says that it is hard to give the right answer when children don't understand the question.

This sitcom isn't far off the mark from testing today. These tests still reflect the test creators' "White bias" and feature prompts that bear little resemblance to the lives of children who are underserved in schools. This explains why certain youth do not perform well on these high-stakes assessments—so named because they serve as gatekeepers. Youth may be labeled, shaped, and controlled by one test score. When I was 22 years old, I remember taking the Miller Analogies Test to get into graduate school, and one test question asked to give an analogous meaning for the word *jihad*. Now culturally, as a Muslim, I know this word means an internal struggle for self-improvement. However, neither this definition nor related language was offered as an option. One of the options, which was scored as correct, was "holy war." But this was incorrect. I felt like getting up and leaving early like Michael. Sadly, these tests become access points for students' futures, and the weight given to them is often unfair.

High-stakes tests create labels, classifications, and segregation of students in schools and classrooms. For example, the SAT (which originally stood for Scholastic Aptitude Test) was first administered in 1926. Given the type of questions asked and the knowledge that was assessed, this assessment was eventually viewed as biased and racist. Rather than resolving the problem, the recent "adversity score" still doesn't address the roots of the historic problem. The adversity score assigns students a ranking of 1 to 100 based on factors related to economic and social difficulties that a student might experience. High-stakes tests still feature unfair, biased measurements of knowledge, intelligence, and learning. These tests are used to further marginalize students who have not been served well by school systems. It's essential that all educators understand the bias and racism prevalent throughout American history so that they can interrupt it each day.

Intellectual Growth

In contrast to this, Black people spoke to the purpose of intellectual growth and the capacity for it. William Watkins, who was born in Baltimore, Maryland, to "free" African American parents (who were also educators), gave a public address on August 8, 1836 to the Moral Reform Society. Watkins was also the cousin of prominent author Frances Ellen Watkins Harper, and studied law while dedicating his life to anti-slavery and abolitionist efforts. The purpose of this Society and their activities was situated in laying out the problems and solutions of racism (Bell, 1958). In his speech, Watkins conceptualizes the importance of education, specifically intellect, and how it should be cultivated among the people. He stated:

> …when the human intellect begins to expand, and put forth its feeble energies, it must be enlightened, strengthened, and disciplined—that when the passions are beginning to be excited by external objects, they must be directed into proper channels; they must be duly regulated; they must be subjected to a judicious moral training; or otherwise the mind, in its development, will be little else than a mental chaos… (Porter, 1995, p. 156)

He goes on to state that the neglect of intellect and the mind is the "most prolific" source of ignorance, which can lead to misery, and "…a suitable education ameliorates the condition of man, renders him a useful member of society, promotes his own happiness, and elevates him to the true dignity of human nature" (Porter, 1995, p. 156). This shows that intellectualism again is connected to happiness, which is the hope of our children and an inalienable right.

Ways to Cultivate Intellect

Teachers' practices of cultivating the intellect should awaken students' interest and genius. Below are some suggested approaches.

Creating an Intellectual Culture

If students are to see themselves as intellectual beings, they must step into schools and classrooms where intellectualism is deeply seeded, expected, and nurtured. Educators must ask themselves the following questions:

- Who is represented (and not represented) on the school and classroom walls?
- Are the school and classroom bright, clean, and organized?
- Is the school or classroom library updated with rich literature and technology that enables critical thought?
- Are there quotes from leading thinkers of the past and present posted around the school and classroom (and taught)?

- Are you open to students critiquing your ideas as the teacher or leader?

- Do you teach students how to critique prudently and unapologetically?

- How are students welcomed each day? Do we speak to students as if they are our respected co-intellectuals?

- How does your teaching text foster intellectual thought and conversation?

- Do you (or your teachers) use prompts and factory-created worksheets? This can inhibit intellectual culture.

- Do you (or your teachers) use packaged curriculum that was not designed for your students' identities? This can also inhibit intellectual culture.

- Who wrote the curriculum your school has adopted? Did experts who share and know the cultural identities of your students and their families design it?

- Are you equally concerned about all students' test scores, or are you more or less concerned about some students' scores?

- What types of professional development do you attend and/or lead? Are they gimmicky, or do they encourage you to read more?

Historicize and Intellectualize Learning Topics

I tell the teachers whom I mentor that I see the world in curriculum. I can walk down the street and "see" lesson plans and how to implement them with youth. In this way, there is so much learning that can be historicized (when you look at the history of something) and intellectualized (when you connect a topic to other learning standards and intellect). A teacher once told me that he wanted to teach about police brutality and wondered if the topic would be taken as "too controversial" by the school principal, and if the principal would see it as being not rigorous enough for teaching. I explained that he just needed to frame the topic in an intellectual light. This often means studying the topic fully and knowing its history and its multiple perspectives. Teachers don't have to push any one perspective on a child; they just have to create a space where children can think across history and develop their own perspectives.

James Baldwin once said, "I love America more than any other country in the world and, exactly for this reason, I insist on the right to criticize her perpetually."

Debate

James Baldwin once said, "I love America more than any other country in the world and, exactly for this reason, I insist on the right to criticize her perpetually." These provocative words always remind me that even the things and ideals that we love and practice should be critiqued. The practice of critique is an intellectual exercise. Critique can also lead to a spirited debate among students in class. It is key that students practice debate as they build intellectual development. Debate allows one to examine a topic through multiple lenses, perspectives or positions.

Sample topics for debate to build classroom or school community:

- Should students attend teachers' and school leaders' planning meetings?
- Should there be police aides in schools?
- Should youth have a say on the selection of curriculum and books?
- Should smartphones be used in the classroom for learning?
- Should schools teach African American studies as a required course of study?

Connect Lesson and Unit Plans
to the Human Condition

The HRL Framework lends benefits and ease of teaching when learning is connected to the human condition or the social and political problems affecting communities. In addition, when learning is connected in this way, it leads to greater intellectualism where students can connect knowledge learned to problem-solving. Learning and working to improve the human condition helps students foster their emotional intelligence and helps to cultivate their hearts. Students can learn and examine social problems and begin to rethink the world in creative ways. To approach learning in this way, teachers can consider what's currently going on in the world and within media and then intellectualize the topic and connect to the skills and standards of the content area. Historically, literary society members always connected their learning to conditions of humanity and never sacrificed this form of intellect for just the learning of skills.

Create Learning Experiences
That Have the "Power of Doing"

James Forten said in a speech I shared earlier that literary societies should have the "power of doing." In much the same way, our classroom spaces and instruction should be tied to action. Students need opportunities to put their learning into action and practice.

Learning and working to improve the human condition helps students foster their emotional intelligence and helps to cultivate their hearts. Students can learn and examine social problems and begin to rethink the world in creative ways.

Teaching Intellectualism as a Learning Pursuit

Teachers need to see themselves as intellectual beings before cultivating the same within the students. Teachers need to believe in the potential of all students regardless of their circumstances or the ways in which adults may have let them down in the past. If teachers focus solely on students' results from one achievement test, they may begin to focus on what students can't do and miss the brilliance that the test may not have captured. There are many negative ways students are represented in media and literature, which can easily condition their minds and thoughts about who they are. I am reminded of the 1940s doll test with Drs. Kenneth and Mamie Clark. This study was intended to study the effects of racism, segregation, and the deficit views of Black people and children. In this study, young Black children were asked to respond to statements while one Black and one White doll lay in front of them. They had to determine or select which doll they preferred. The results were that these children did not carry the highest esteem for their race due to social conditioning. The conditions of society greatly harmed the inner spirits and minds of young Black youth. This proved the power of oppressive agendas and one of the causes of anti-Blackness.

As we consider classrooms today, educators must be aware that previous social conditioning isn't just a thing of the past but still manifests today. If a society tells children they aren't good enough through television, songs, cartoons, or other forms of media, they may still think they aren't capable of the intellectualism I am describing in the book. Additionally, this is exacerbated when teacher education programs and K–12 classrooms do not explicitly teach Black and Brown excellence. And I'm not just talking about teaching this excellence during one month of the school year—this excellence needs to be embedded in the culture and fabric of the school. Culture, race, and cultural responsiveness cannot be packaged in a program or restricted time frame. One principal of a school that I worked with told the students that if they were to have a month celebrating the heritage of Black history, then they needed to also have a White history month. Clearly, this principal is ignorant of much of U.S. history and lacks a deep understanding of the needs of all children. Students need to feel valued and loved. They need to know that they matter to all adults in the school. And they need to know they are capable of the intellectual greatness their ancestors practiced and promoted. This means teachers need to create a space of intellectualism where students see themselves as the next generation of thinkers. This will come through in their language use, topics taught, and the texts they engage in. This will help with the level of anti-intellectualism that we still have in schools. Evidence of anti-intellectualism is seen in the following examples in schools and classrooms:

- The prescribed and packaged curriculum with scripts for teaching
- The over-reliance of testing of objective knowledge of skills
- The leveling of texts and tracking of students
- The invisibility or lack of truths of the country's oppression and enslavement
- The constraint teachers have with curriculum they are being told to teach with
- The lack of intellectual and cultural diversity within children's literature
- The lack of "teacher as intellectual" with classroom observations and evaluation
- The lack of planning time teachers have for innovation and creation of curriculum
- The lack of intellectual thought held in the texts teachers are asked to teach

Herb Kohl (1983) wrote:

> An intellectual is someone who knows about his or her field, has a wide breadth of knowledge about other aspects of the world, who uses experience to develop theory and questions theory on the basis of further experience. An intellectual is also someone who has the courage to question authority and who refuses to act counter to his or her own experience and judgment (Giroux, 30).

And we must think about whether teacher education programs encourage the intellectualism of teachers in their disciplines, or merely push the teaching through "tool kits" or a handful of strategies. The teacher as the intellectual knows the theories of the world and of the profession, as every problem in education can be explained by analyzing the right theories (Love, 2019). This type of teacher could then see the brilliance in the minds of their students and hopefully teach to only cultivate their intellect.

Lesson Sample

Identity: Students will learn the significance of water to living a healthy life and examine the water quality in their communities. (*environmental identity*)

Skills:

- **English Language Arts:** Students will cite textual evidence to support analysis of what the text says explicitly as well as inferences drawn from the text.
- **Math:** Students will be able to understand the concept of a ratio and use ratio language to describe the relationships between lead poisoning, race, and income.
- **Science:** Students will define environmental justice and name the importance of water quality for humans.
- **Social Studies:** Students will investigate the history of water and its significance to civilizations throughout time.

Intellect: Students will examine the concept of marginalization and investigate the water crisis in Flint, Michigan.

Criticality: Students will identify ways in which the state government made decisions regarding the source and treatment of Flint's drinking water and the oppression/marginalization that such decisions caused.

Intellectualism should not be minimized. It can't be taught by just teaching the textbook or packaged curricular programs; it requires ingenuity and creativity from the teacher and the school leaders. The genius, intellect, and brilliance of students are within them. Teachers need to cultivate and "water" it so that students can lead a full and joyous life when they leave our schools.

Questions for Further Consideration: Teachers and Preservice Teachers

1. What are you currently reading to help advance and stimulate your mind?

2. In what ways are your students and their parents brilliant?

3. Do you identify as an intellectual? How do you enact intellectualism in your personal and professional life?

4. When learning the history of education in your professional development, whose intellectual histories are included, and whose are left out? How did/does this learning affect the ways in which you teach? Whose intellectual histories do you teach in math, science, English language arts, and social studies?

5. What is the meaning and history of the discipline you teach? What are mathematics, science, English language arts, and social studies? What is the history of your content area across different eras? Why is *arts* coupled with the word *language*? Why is *social* coupled with *studies*? How would you teach a lesson plan on your discipline to your students using the HRL Framework?

Questions for Further Consideration: Principals and School Leaders

1. How do you cultivate an intellectual school culture for the teachers, parents, and students in your leadership?

2. What intellectual data do you collect about the students? How is this data used to inform your leadership?

3. What programs and initiatives do you plan that allow students to put their knowledge into action?

4. How do you use your school budget for classroom books that are intellectually and culturally diverse?

5. What interview questions do you ask to gauge potentially hired teachers' intellectualism and their capacity to cultivate students' intellect?

Toward the Pursuit of Criticality

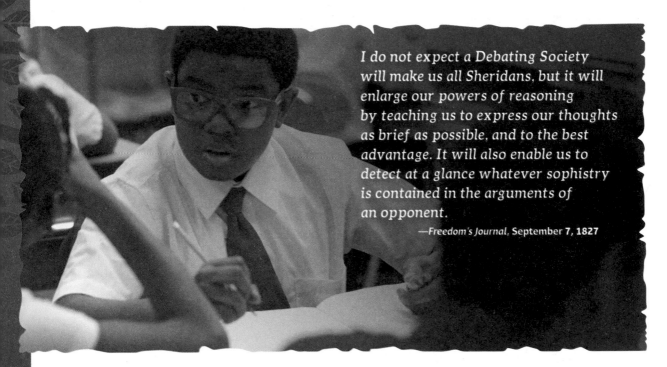

I do not expect a Debating Society will make us all Sheridans, but it will enlarge our powers of reasoning by teaching us to express our thoughts as brief as possible, and to the best advantage. It will also enable us to detect at a glance whatever sophistry is contained in the arguments of an opponent.

—*Freedom's Journal,* September 7, 1827

The excerpt above comes from *Freedom's Journal* on September 7, 1827. The excerpt, written by "A Young Man," states a central purpose of literary or debating societies, which is (1) to enlarge powers of reasoning, (2) to express thoughts briefly and to the best advantage to an audience, and 3) to detect sophistry or falsehood or fallacies contained in the language of others—in other words, putting intellect into action. The aim is to detect or recognize misrepresentations or deceptiveness in the language of the opponent or those who challenge truths. And this brings us to the concept of "criticality"—reading print texts and contexts with an understanding of how power, anti-oppression, and equity operates throughout society. Criticality enables us to question both the world and texts within it to better understand the truth in history, power, and equity.

Understanding Criticality

When I introduce criticality to teachers, it is often a new concept for them, especially when they have not learned critical theories related to race, gender, class, or anti-oppression in their formal teacher education preparation. Critical theories that are helpful for educators include critical race theory, Black feminist theory, and LatCrit. These theories (as examples) express the importance of using frameworks to understand racial and other disparities. The theories also help teachers develop a critical lens on the world and on their teaching. Criticality helps teachers understand and explain inequities in education and is a step toward teaching anti-oppression, something that may not be in the forefront of teachers' minds as they are encouraged to focus on test prep, college and career readiness, or skills-centered instruction. These elements of education alone can be very damaging for youth, especially for Black youth who are often told that they aren't good enough and are treated violently in their own communities.

Criticality enables us to question both the world and texts within it to better understand the truth in history, power, and equity.

Teaching criticality humanizes instruction and makes it more compassionate. Although it's reprehensible that we even have to remind educators to humanize their approach toward youth of color—as a thoughtful and humanistic stance should be organic to all of humankind—this speaks to a history of unequal and inequitable treatment in schools. I also explain criticality through a poem, written in the year 1258, in which humanness was expressed in a few simple lines. Written by the Persian poet Sa'di, the prose poem called *The Gulistan of Sa'di* is especially dear to me because I was named after this influential work and poetry has always been my most beloved genre. The "Ghul" sound of *The Gulistan* is reflected in my name and means "the rose garden."

Sa'di is best known for writing Persian literature about gardens and roses. His poetry is uniquely grounded in knowledge and wisdom. And although this particular poem was written over 760 years ago, it's still significant today. An English translation is written:

> Human race are members of one frame, since all, at first,
> came from the same essence, when by hard fortune one limb
> is oppressed the other members lose their wonted rest,
> if thou feels not for others' misery, thou don't deserve
> to be called Human (Chapter 1, Story 10).

Sa'di reminds us that human beings are both members of a whole and part of one essence. In this regard, if one member of the collective whole is afflicted with pain, then other people within humanity should also experience pain. In other words, "human" represents one body, and each particular group of people is a unique arm of humanity, such as Black lives, so-called immigrants (so-called, because to whom does the land really belong?), women, students with IEPs, Latinx students, Muslims, or others. If that arm or group of people is wounded, oppressed, or hurt, and if the other parts of the body or members of society are apathetic and do nothing to respond to others' pain, then they don't deserve to be called human. Empathy is the essence of what it means to be human. Now, this is a powerful assertion. Sa'di pushes us to ask ourselves, "What does it mean to be human? What is personal responsibility in the face of human violence and oppression? What do humanizing practices look like in and outside of the classroom?"

What does it mean to be human? What is personal responsibility in the face of human violence and oppression? What do humanizing practices look like in and outside of the classroom?

These are the questions criticality begins to address. And the last question, "What do humanizing practices look like in and outside of the classroom?" is also essential, because it speaks to those "social justice" educators who leave the school and don't live in anti-racist, anti-sexist, and other anti-oppressive ways in their daily lives. This is why we must not just be non-racist or non-oppressive but also work with passion and diligence to actively disrupt oppression in and outside of the classroom. Simple good intentions aren't enough. The intentions must be deliberately connected to actions.

We have too many recurring news headlines of the mistreatment and marginalization of youth of color in schools across the nation. In just the last few years alone, we read about teachers dressing up for Halloween as "Mexicans" and "border walls," simulating slave auctions, and sending notes home to Black parents requesting that they not teach their daughters to have Black girl magic. In other news, we learn of Black girls being strip-searched at school for laughing too loud, or teachers asking Black students to lie on the floor to experience what slavery feels like. This unfortunately doesn't even begin to address all the foolishness that happens in schools—led by teachers who don't carry love for their students' consciousness or criticality. This school-based trauma should incite widespread outrage. Teachers, administrators, parents, school board members, politicians, and all concerned citizens should be furious at this injustice. If we responded to all forms of mistreatment and harm to students with the same anger that was directed toward teachers caught cheating on a state test, we could come closer to creating the schools that students deserve. But currently, most of us look the other way while youth are systematically stripped of their identities, histories, joy, and civil rights in our schools. Criticality begins to give students the tools to respond to injustice in and around schools.

What Is Criticality?

Criticality is the capacity to read, write, and think in ways of understanding power, privilege, social justice, and oppression, particularly for populations who have been historically marginalized in the world (Muhammad, 2018). When youth have criticality, they are able to see, name, and interrogate the world not only to make sense of injustice but also to work toward social transformation. Thus, students need spaces to name and critique injustice and ultimately have the agency to build a better world for all.

When youth have criticality, they are able to see, name, and interrogate the world not only to make sense of injustice but also to work toward social transformation.

As long as oppression is present in the world, students need pedagogy that nurtures criticality. And we have never had a world free from oppression. I differentiate between lowercase c *critical* and uppercase C *Critical* when defining criticality. While *critical* means to think deeply about something, *Critical* is connected to an understanding of power, entitlement, oppression, and equity.

Criticality calls for teachers and students to understand the ideologies and perspectives of marginalized communities (especially Black populations all over the world) and their ways of knowing and experiencing the world. Without this knowledge and anti-oppressive beliefs of their own, it becomes impossible to teach criticality in the classroom because it calls for a direct interruption of the things that disturb peace in the world and in communities. Educators must think outside of themselves, including the cultural identities and values that they have come to know and believe. Criticality is feeling for those who are not treated in humane ways regardless of what the law, policy, and norms dictate. Enslavement was still wrong even though we had laws that said it was right and good. If we consider this history, we know that we still have policies and laws in place that cause some people to be killed, persecuted, or treated in inhumane ways. Do we follow these policies just because they are written in print, or do we interrogate them and teach students to create a better world for all people—including those who look different from them?

Criticality helps students to tell the difference between facts and truths. Oftentimes, facts do not capture the full narrative of people but are taught in schools as the histories of people of color. Truths, in turn, are the realities and lived experiences of persons experiencing the moment, which equally contribute to the same narrative (Brown, 2013). For example, let's consider the Black girl at Spring Valley High School in South Carolina who was thrown around in her seat and physically abused by the school police officer. She was violently dragged across the room and assaulted because it was reported that the student did not put her cell phone away in the classroom. We rarely, however, see students' truths in such reports. This girl's truths could be that she was not loved or valued in the school—that she was nervous or embarrassed—that she did not feel that the curriculum responded to her identities. If we just focused on the fact that she did not abide by a cell phone policy, we miss the fullness of students' experiences. We miss the truths in people of color's experiences. Regardless, this did not warrant a physical assault on a child and shows again how Black children and their bodies are devalued. Truths move toward listening and honoring the voices of the marginalized person. Therefore, a push for criticality in learning standards is helping young people, including those from backgrounds that have not been historically marginalized, to investigate positions from different standpoints. Examining text and concepts through different perspectives and standpoints is an intellectual task.

Advancing criticality pushes students to cultivate the tools to dismantle deficit ways of the world and to protect themselves against wrongdoing (Ginwright & James, 2002). They learn the historical, institutional, and structural elements that shape the world and that explain why forms of oppression exist. One fallacy is that criticality is only for Black and Brown people, or others who have been oppressed across the world. This isn't true. Black and Brown people have historically been the oppressed across many lands. And we didn't create situations that caused us to be oppressed. This is similar to thinking that culturally and historically responsive education is only for African American or Latinx students. This is a false and limited way of viewing education, similar to suggesting that greatness is only reserved for African American or Latinx students. Perhaps the people who need criticality the most become those who share identities with the greatest oppressors of the world. But in truth, given the complex identities of youth, all students and teachers need culturally and historically responsive education.

Other associations with criticality include:

- Being woke
- Knowledge of how to navigate racist systems
- A deep social awareness of injustice
- Knowledge of systems and structures that cause failure
- Understanding power and power dynamics
- Understanding what it means to be Black and Brown in the world
- Understanding the marginality of others who look like us and are different

In short, teaching criticality helps students assume responsibility for the ways in which they process information—to avoid being passive consumers of knowledge and information. Criticality helps students read the world with a critical eye, refusing to accept unexamined information as factual or true. As an example, I ask teachers to think about a song they may have listened to during their youth and then relisten to the song today with a Critical ear. They are likely to hear the lyrics differently. This experience may prompt us to ask, *Who allowed us to listen to that song?* (especially if our adult self now finds the lyrics inappropriate). When we see youth listening to songs or taking in the content of some video games, it becomes problematic if they are not consuming this media with criticality. Criticality pushes questioning of information and the source of the information—and this source may include the teachers. Therefore, criticality (like culturally relevant/responsive pedagogies) does not believe in hierarchies in teaching and learning. Instead, the knowledge and perspectives students bring is honored and valued, and the classroom becomes a community of teachers and learners. We all can make more informed decisions when we have

Criticality helps students read the world with a critical eye, refusing to accept unexamined information as factual or truth.

criticality. Our students will grow older and vote, have relationships with others, and decide where they spend their money. Criticality allows for discernment to make positive decisions that are healthy for them and their communities.

Criticality and Other Literacies

Criticality has a direct connection to the other literacies, specifically *critical literacy*, *racial literacy*, and *agitation literacies*.

Critical Literacy

Critical literacy refers to reading, writing, and thinking in active and reflective ways with goals of understanding power, inequality, oppression, and social justice and investigating multiple perspectives and questioning and reading between the lines of the text (Beck, 2005; Giroux, 1987; Luke, 2000). This is in opposition to passive learning, where there is typically one correct answer and students are not encouraged to take multiple meanings from the content learning. Part of critical literacy and criticality is for students to gain print authority, which is defined as understanding a topic so well that they can critique the topic and offer their own perspectives and opinions. This is why criticality must first ground learning in students' identities—and, in this way, provide the access needed to teach skills and proficiencies.

Racial Literacy

Racial literacy is the capability of seeing, naming, and interpreting the world with a Critical lens, where one is keenly aware of race. Omi and Winant (1994) conceptualize race as "a concept which signifies and symbolizes social conflicts and interests by referring to different types of human bodies" (p. 55). Racial literacy is essential in our current sociocultural and political environment since race is socially constructed. Race is a complex phenomenon and involves an intricate analysis of history, hegemony, and power as a starting point for understanding. Racial literacy is the understanding and enactments of reading, writing, speaking, and thinking of race in regard to its impact on "social, economic, political, and educational experiences of individuals and groups" (Skerrett, 2011, p. 314). In this way, developing racial literacy also entails deciphering the racialized structures and hierarchies of the world (Guiner, 2004; Sealey-Ruiz, 2013), thus making one better prepared to navigate racism that is projected onto self and/or others. Due to a history of being pathologized and relegated based on social constructions of race and racism, it is critical for young people to be racially literate. Although racism is one type of oppression, and the goal of criticality addresses multiple oppressions, race and racism are typically embedded and layered with other oppressions like sexism, homophobia, ageism, classism, and religious discrimination.

Researchers and educators around the country, concerned about the ways in which schools are failing to meet the needs of students of color, are creating spaces for teachers and community members to have conversations about race and racial violence. This includes school districts that have a reputation of high achievement and strong academics. These same districts do not always have data to show high achievement and academics for Black students. People should ask themselves, "How comfortable am I with talking about race and addressing the disparities in my school?" Some teachers struggle with saying "Black lives matter" out loud, and yet they teach Black students. This will not work. Such teachers can never be effective or highly qualified. I ask, why do people have a hard time talking about race if they are doing right by all students?

Agitation Literacies

Agitation literacies are ways of reading, writing, thinking, and speaking that are connected to the intention and action to upset, disturb, disquiet, and unhinge systemic oppression (Muhammad, 2019). Frederick Douglass addressed this concept in a public address on August 3, 1857. In this speech, entitled, "West India Emancipation," Douglass states:

> Let me give you a word of the philosophy of reform. The whole history of the progress of human liberty shows that all concessions, yet made to her august claims, have been born of earnest struggle. The conflict has been exciting, agitating, all-absorbing, and for the time being putting all other tumults to silence. It must do this or it does nothing. If there is no struggle, there is no progress. Those who profess to favor freedom, and yet depreciate agitation, are men who want crops without plowing up the ground.... They want the ocean without the awful roar of its many waters. This struggle may be a moral one; or it may be a physical one; or it may be both moral and physical, but it must be a struggle. Power concedes nothing without a demand. It never did and it never will. Find out just what any people will quietly submit to and you have found out the exact measure of injustice and wrong which will be imposed upon them, and these will continue till they are resisted with either words or blows, or with both.
>
> —Frederick Douglass, 1857

In this speech, Douglass addresses the urgency of freedom for enslaved people and calls attention to the philosophy undergirding reform. Reform, as he implicitly defines it in the fuller speech, is unconfined and only attained when those who desire freedom will *inconvenience* themselves and ensure others gain the same freedom they desire for themselves. Further, Douglass asserts that freedom through reform is only reached when our thoughts (or words) are explicitly linked to action. In his writing, he speaks to the critical role of enslaved people and the necessity that they engage in social action—through resistance and agitation.

In another example, Ida B. Wells-Barnett wrote a letter on January 1, 1902 to the Anti-Lynching Bureau outlining the urgency to respond to the terrorist acts of violence projected on the lives of Black women and men. She stated that 135 human beings met death at the hands of lynching mobs in the last year, and she consequently used her pen in unapologetic ways to bring light and attention to these horrific crimes. Through her writing, she further urged members to agitate—to trouble the waters and disrupt oppression.

> To the Members of the Anti-Lynching Bureau:
>
> …the need for agitation and publication of facts is greater than ever, while the avenues through which to make such publications have decreased.…When the bureau was first organized three years ago, it was thought that every man, woman, and child who had a drop of Negro blood in his veins and every person else who wanted to see mob law put down would gladly contribute 25 cents per year to this end.… Nevertheless my faith in the justice of our cause and the absolute need of this agitation leads me to again address those who have shown 25 cents worth of interest in the matter heretofore.…In view of the recent agitation in Congress and out anent the disfranchisement of the Negro and the causes alleged therefore it was thought best to throw some light on those times and give some unwritten history.

This was not the first or last time where Black writers used their pens to agitate. In my study of historical archives of the writings of Black people, I find the words *agitate* and *agitation* throughout their literary writings from the 19th century onward. They enacted literacies to define their identities, resist oppression, and to promote social change. In this way, they weren't just readers or writers, but they also practiced criticality and were activists working toward a better humanity. The need to agitate for criticality historically spoke to the social unrest at the time, and I argue that the need to agitate is still necessary and pressing in classrooms today.

Ways to Learn, Understand, and Teach Criticality

Teachers' practices of cultivating criticality should help students read the world. Below are some suggested approaches.

Introduce Self Through Critical Texts

Have students introduce themselves through a piece of text that speaks to their ideologies, sociopolitical beliefs, and values. This text can be an image, social media text, print, or video. This should speak to how they define their own consciousness and should become a helpful way to get to know the thinking and perspectives of students. This historically responsive practice speaks to the importance of text and the power of language. Guiding questions for teachers include:

- What piece of text/book speaks to how you view injustice in the world?
- Why did you select this text to help others know who you are and what you believe?
- How does this text connect to who you are and what you believe?
- What beliefs are contrary to those expressed in your selected text?
- If you were to write a commentary piece to your selected text, what would you write?

Preamble Writing

A preamble is a preliminary or introductory statement. Writing a preamble was a historical practice in Black literary societies throughout the 19th century. In an example from the 1831 Black women's literary society, The Female Literary Association of Philadelphia, the young women wrote:

> Conscious that among the various pursuits that have engaged the attention of mankind in the different eras of the world, none have ever been considered, by persons of judgment and penetration, as superior to the cultivation of the intellectual powers bestowed upon us by the God of nature. It therefore becomes a duty

incumbent upon us as women, as daughters of a despised race, to use our utmost endeavors to enlighten the understanding, to cultivate the talents entrusted to our keeping, that by so doing, we may in a great measure, break down the strong behavior of prejudice, and raise ourselves to an equality with those of our fellow beings, who differ from us in complexion, but who are with ourselves, children of one Eternal Parent, and by his immutatable law, we are entitled to the same rights and privileges; therefore, we, whose names are hereunto subscribed, do agree to form ourselves into a society for the promotion of this great object, to be called 'The Female Literary Association of Philadelphia.'

These preambles become powerful statements of intention and objective. As teachers start the school year, they can ask students to collectively compose their classroom community manifesto or statement that speaks to the purpose and power of their engagement in mathematics, science, social studies, or writing. This statement is then read every day in unison (standing) to start and conclude the class. When students embrace this exercise, they begin to engage in the learning because they are the ones who are establishing the purpose for both teaching and learning, rather than others who have never met them (those who construct standards for learning). They also find value in having their voices heard and on record. I start by asking students to write statements that speak to what they seek to learn from our class and why our content learning is key. I ask them to be clear and bold in their statements. I then ask each student to read their statements as I project them on the screen for all to see. As a class, they collectively decide on the final draft. Each student has to agree on the preamble.

Here is a sample of young boys' and girls' (ages 10 to 17) preamble:

> **We, the Brother and Sister Authors,** free our Black minds for the past, present, and future. We choose to write our stories to show who we really are with our voices high and our pens in our hands. We shall come forth as one to show others what we were built for, as we strive to break down the barriers from the unjust and unloving societies. With respect for each other and for our Blackness, we are all equal when we pick up our pens.

While taking pride in every word, we will leave behind an imprint with every pen stroke.

As the educator, I must respond to my students' needs within the design of my curriculum and instruction. In the same way, I usually engage teachers in this same exercise so they are reminded of the purpose and power of their teaching.

Here is a sample preamble from a group of teachers I worked with recently across New York City Schools and NYC Men Teach:

> **We, the Historically Responsive Teachers,** teach to liberate others. Because of others' beliefs in us, we know our possibilities are endless. We teach to see change in the world, especially when the world rejects it. If we can be that beacon for a child to tap into their uninhibited agency, then our presence has value. Teaching in its true essence is a labor of love. Teaching is to empower and help nurture the innate drive for self-actualization. We are here to rebel from the status quo as we teach students to respond to their worlds, relate to what they learn and reflect on how they will transform the world. We teach to feed students' curiosity, so that we can lift as we climb together.

If we study the language across all preambles, we learn the importance of teaching and learning. Notice that neither of these express the goal of passing high-stakes tests or grades. This was never the focus; instead, if we examine the language closely, these preambles purposefully concentrated on identity, skills, intellect, and criticality. And by way of these goals, the writers of these statements are able to achieve other successes.

Interrogation of Media

Bring in current or historical examples of media for students to examine. The media has, over time, conditioned the minds and hearts of the public and, in one way or another, contributed to the marginalization of various groups. Students are encouraged to interrogate these documents to understand how racism and other oppressions have been in existence over time, which helps us to understand the current sociopolitical landscape.

Fifteen Demands of Education

Similar to the group of high school students who wrote and published 15 demands of their education in the *Black News*, teachers can also ask students ways they would like their education and school to improve (see page 43). This historical artifact can be read by students today to see how far we have come and how much still remains to be done. Collectively, students can continue the historical tradition of writing out their needs and demands and making it public for others to read and move toward action. When we study the demands of Black students from 1969, we find that the youth at that time taught adults how to "get it right." The question becomes, "Have we listened? Have we moved toward their suggested changes? And whose best interest has education served from 1969 to today?" Students can then historicize and intellectualize their demands and move them toward action.

Critical Open Letters

When I work with students, I have them pen open letters to future generations of youth across sociopolitical issues that are important to their lives. This practice is a part of a rich literary tradition of Black people (Newkirk, 2009). Historically, African Americans have written letters across diverse topics of love, justice, and education, to name

[From the New York Observer.]

A LIBRARY FOR THE PEOPLE OF COLOR.

MESSRS. EDITORS:—Aware that you take a lively interest in the subject of the improvement and elevation of our colored population, I am free to address you in behalf of a Library and Reading Room lately opened by the executive committee of the Phœnix Society, for their benefit.

The institution is located in spacious rooms, second story of the north-west corner of Canal and Mercer streets. Connected with it, is a classic school of ten or twelve promising youth. Much good, it is hoped, will result from the successful prosecution of the purposes of this establishment.

The establishment of schools, of libraries, of reading rooms, and the delivery of public lectures for our benefit, I trust will be seed sown in good ground.

Some among us are poor, and ignorant, and vicious, *because we have been neglected.* The time has come, in which we sincerely hope our community will not stop to find fault with our oppressed people, but turn their attention to their education, and to the improvement of their condition. Permit me, therefore, through your useful paper, to solicit donations from the favored citizens of New York, in books, maps, papers, money, &c. for the benefit of our feeble institution. And I would beg the benevolent ladies of our city, who are first in every good work, *not to forget us.* We shall thankfully receive from them any volumes they may have read and laid by, or any useful papers they can dispense with. We hope to be the objects of some of the ten thousand acts of daily benevolence; and we will promise, in return, to bestow on our benefactors the blessing of thousands ready to perish.

The objects of the institution are general improvement, and the training of our youth to habits of reading and reflection.

I need not tell you that, for the want of such institutions, many of the young and unthinking part of our colored citizens are led by those older than themselves to haunts of wickedness and vice. Many young men, yea! and old ones too, spend their evenings in improper places, because they have no public libraries, no reading rooms, nor useful lectures, to attract their attention, and occupy their leisure hours. We hope to save such from ruin, and lead them to habits of virtue and usefulness.

Letter written by abolitionist and journalist Samuel E. Cornish to the editors of *The New York Observer*, December 7, 1833, a few. In these letters, Black people wrote to resist some form of injustice. In one such letter, written about one of the literary societies on December 7, 1833, abolitionist and journalist Samuel E. Cornish writes to the editors of *The New York Observer* on behalf of the Library and Reading Room and Phoenix Society. Cornish argues for the urgent establishment of schools, literary societies, and libraries to counter the neglect of Black people. He calls for improved educational conditions and ways for young people to access spaces for learning so they can spend their time reading and cultivating their minds. Letter writing is an art form and could help to inspire future generations in overcoming adversity. Teachers can ask students to write these at the end of the year, and the incoming group of students could then read the letters the following year.

Teaching Criticality as a Learning Pursuit

If teachers engage in the teaching of criticality, it is necessary that they assume an active and critical stance in their own lives. It is impossible to teach students to have a Critical lens if teachers don't have one themselves. Teaching criticality asks, "How will I engage students' thinking about power, anti-oppression, and equity in the text, in communities, and in society?" Teachers and students together can then think of topics, social problems, or important issues embedded with power and (in)justice. This becomes a springboard for designing curriculum for learning. Teachers must also look at their current curriculum and ask how they can explore issues of power, access, and equity within. With deep thinking and knowledge, one can think about how goals of criticality align with the content learning.

Lesson Sample

Identity: Students will consider their own preference for roller coasters and amusement parks. (*risk or thrill identity*)

Skills:

- **English Language Arts:** Students will determine two or more main ideas of a text and explain how they are supported by key details; summarize the text.

- **Math:** Students will graph proportional relationships, interpreting the unit rate as the slope of the graph, and compare different proportional relationships represented in different ways.

- **Science:** Students will learn about the kinetic energy of roller coasters.

- **Social Studies:** Students will learn the history and context of amusement parks.

Intellect: Students will learn about the history of the first roller coaster and the timeline of its evolution.

Criticality: Students will learn about the segregation of amusement parks and other recreational facilities.

Criticality is not just something that is fun or interesting to do at the end of the semester as a time filler. It is an intellectual practice of studying the state of humanity. Criticality isn't taught as an add-on to any topic. It is ongoing and needs to be discussed and cultivated constantly within all of us. Students need to leave teachers' classrooms with a stronger sense of criticality in order to survive and thrive in the world. They also must learn to live in a world with others who may not share their racial, gender, or other identities. And we want to make sure our youth become future adults who will work toward humanization and not perpetuate oppressions.

Questions for Further Consideration: Teachers and Preservice Teachers

1. How have others profited from the failure of Black and Brown youth?

2. In one word, how would you describe the current social times in which we live? How could this word translate into a lesson plan or learning opportunity for students? In other words, how could you translate this word into content learning?

3. How do you actively teach about and disrupt oppression in your teaching?

4. When you establish criticality as a learning goal, what do you do well or with excellence and what do you need to improve upon?

5. What social issues connect to the quality of life for your students? How can you put this into a math, science, English language arts, or social studies lesson plan?

Questions for Further Consideration: Principals and School Leaders

1. How often do you talk about race and racism with your staff? How do you begin these conversations?

2. Are you okay with ongoing healing and support toward critical issues, or do you expect resolutions in each conversation with your staff? Do teachers and staff see you as an agitator toward righteousness for all?

3. Name ways you enact anti-racism in your leadership (not just non-racism).

4. How can you build opportunities where students are on committees for teacher interviews, curriculum selection, and school policies?

5. When incidents occur regarding student behavior, do you first examine structures and systems that could have caused the event to happen? Are policies written to prevent misbehavior or just to punish students?

Implementing Historically Responsive Texts and Lesson Plans

Part Three of this book, Chapters 7 and 8, focuses on the importance of cultivating libraries and selecting historically responsive texts for teaching. Chapter 7 provides a historical account of the importance of books and literature, and how these were used as vehicles to further their purpose in literary societies. Chapter 8 gives readers a lesson plan template and more sample lessons and unit plans that are inclusive of the four-layered equity pursuits of Historically Responsive Literacy.

CHAPTER 7

Selecting Historically Responsive Texts

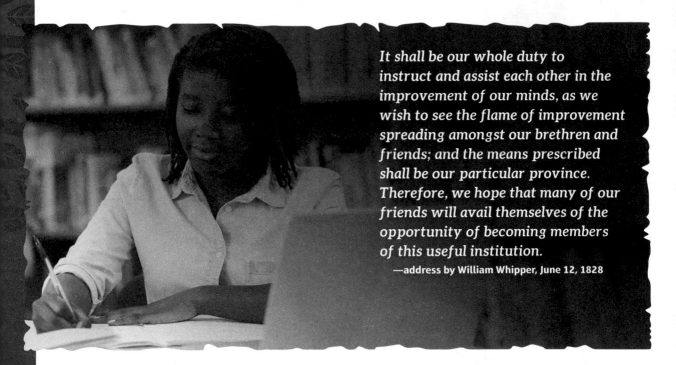

It shall be our whole duty to instruct and assist each other in the improvement of our minds, as we wish to see the flame of improvement spreading amongst our brethren and friends; and the means prescribed shall be our particular province. Therefore, we hope that many of our friends will avail themselves of the opportunity of becoming members of this useful institution.

—address by William Whipper, June 12, 1828

On the evening of June 12, 1828, William Whipper addressed the Colored Reading Society of Philadelphia for Mental Improvement. In the fuller address, he opened with the usefulness of society members to cherish and focus on their "moral and intellectual improvement." He spoke on the importance of establishing such an organization to understand the past, but also to help with future advancement. He reminded the society they were living in the golden age of literature and learning, and that an institution like this one would be helpful for erudition. In the excerpt here, he named the vehicle for all learning—books. He stated that members must pay monthly fees and that monies spent on "useful books" would be in the care of the society's librarian. Interestingly, the members were set to meet once a week to return books and check out books. During this meeting, those returning books were expected to share whatever learning or sentiments they gained from the book they read as a way to help other members understand the content and consider whether they wanted to read and subsequently check out the same book. The seventh stipulation outlined the central purpose of societies, libraries, and books, which entailed collaborative knowledge sharing rather than selfishly keeping education to oneself. Whipper explained: "It shall be our whole duty to instruct and assist each other in the improvement of our minds," speaking to the sociocentric nature and collective responsibility of members of these spaces.

Books mattered. In literary societies, literature and reading various texts were at the heart of all their pursuits and literacy learning goals. They read diverse literature to enrich their minds and also to cultivate their identities, skills, intellect, and criticality. When they had funds, they put all their money into the establishment of libraries and their book collections. Today, we find libraries in and out of schools underfunded and bare. Even classroom libraries, where students should be able to check out books and share sentiments about the texts, are scarce. This is especially true in higher grades and content areas that are not English language arts or literature classes. As a school district administrator, I once observed an entire school erected from the ground up, and the last thing they added, almost as an afterthought, was a library. Again, this was in conflict with the students' histories. This school library was little more than a few shelves in a small room, while historically, the library was considered the heart of the school. Indeed, the school was constructed around the library; it was not the last room to be considered.

"It shall be our whole duty to instruct and assist each other in the improvement of our minds..."

Defining Text

I define *text* as anything that can be read—both print texts and nonprint texts. Society members were reading print texts, but they were also reading the world as texts (Freire & Macedo, 1987). They read images and the social times as texts. In this chapter, I describe the cultivation and purpose of libraries during this time and how they used texts to advance the four layers of the HRL Framework. I then offer some practical lesson and unit plans using the HRL model. We know that books matter; so, too, do the representation and diversity of thought reflected in the content of books. The lack of diversity available in the books teachers are given to teach with remains a challenge. As in the wider media (television, film, and advertisements), there is a shortage of representation of people of color in children's literature. Most of the children's books published do not represent people of color or their experiences. Moreover, books with diverse characters are not widely written by authors of color. Oftentimes, books that children read and their stories/histories are told by White authors. In 2018, the Cooperative Children's Book Center, School of Education at the University of Wisconsin-Madison, collected statistics on the diversity of children's book depicting characters from diverse backgrounds. They found that 1 percent of books represented American Indians/First Nations; 5 percent represented Latinx populations;

7 percent represented Asian Pacific Islander/Asian Pacific American; and 10 percent of books presented African or African American. Meanwhile, 27 percent of books represented animals or others and 50 percent of books represented White characters (Huyck, Dahlen & Dahlen, 2019). This becomes a problem for book publishers and all those who decide who or what to publish and not publish. The stories and authors of color are there. Therefore, we need more diversity in texts in and out of classrooms and also access to other literature when the school-sanctioned literature isn't enough.

We need more diversity in texts in and out of classrooms and also access to other literature when the school-sanctioned literature isn't enough.

Students are disconnected from texts in and out of schools for a number of reasons, including the following:

- Unchanged, White-centered curriculum (including the characters and stories)
- The gap between research from children's-literature scholars and texts used in the classroom
- Students are not involved with textual selections
- Lack of diversity in representation, authorship, and thought
- The texts are not responsive to students' identities, histories, and literacies
- Students don't find texts to be significant or meaningful, or the teacher does not find connections to students' lives
- Students and teachers are deprived of textual lineages (Tatum, 2009)
- Lack of multimodal texts paired with traditional print texts
- Unclear purpose of pursuits of reading
- Disconnect with other pursuits of literacy (writing, debating, speaking, performance, etc.)
- Texts are typically selected to respond to or intended to cultivate skills only

Below, I detail two major sources of texts that historically allowed for the pursuit of the HRL learning goals—libraries and Black newspapers. Each offers great lessons as we strive to diversify texts today and provide teaching and learning where students see themselves, not just White stories, histories, or images. Early Black readers didn't just read from Black authors, but maintained a diversity of authorship. Historically, texts featured news stories of the nation as well as international literature. In the historical artifact here, published in *The Elevator* on September 8, 1865, the language shows that African Americans held papers and readings from all over the world.

> **Our Reading-Room.**
>
> We intend connecting with our Reading-Room a Course of Lectures on miscellaneous subjects, to be delivered monthly,—perhaps oftener. We also contemplate establishing a Library. To all of which subscribers will have access without extra charge. We will have on our files papers from all parts of the world.

A historical artifact published in
The Elevator on September 8, 1865

Literary Society Libraries

Literary society members developed libraries to furnish texts. The library was the heart and soul of each literary society and provided the literature and reading materials to push an agenda for cultivating a generation of literate beings who were able to read the word and the world. The significance of libraries was recognized as the energy of these societies. In 1827, before the first literary society, *Freedom's Journal* printed an extensive column devoted to the benefit of libraries across communities:

> Of many made by friends of learning in different parts of the Globe, none have met [sic] with more success, nor been attended with more benefits to the community at large, than the establishment, in different cities towns, and villages, of libraries: whether we consider them as public, social, or private.

Libraries were essential for creating a just society. Each society would work to furnish its libraries with genres of international texts that offered topics on political issues, as well as works about love, faith, and the spirit of hope.

In 1833, The Library Company of Colored Persons exemplified this same central focus on the development of libraries. Founded by 10 men, including William Whipper of the Reading Room Society, this society was "deeply impressed with the necessity of promoting among our rising youth, a proper cultivation for literary pursuits and the improvement of the faculties and powers of their minds" (Porter, 1936). This became their preamble. To this end, the Library Company's main objective was to build a library collection of "useful works of every description for the benefit of its members, who might there successfully apply without comparatively any cost, for that mental good which they could not readily obtain elsewhere." The society soon accumulated a collection of reading materials such as books, pamphlets, and maps through donations, which helped to accomplish the goals of literacy development of the organization. They authorized specific members to receive books and other donations on behalf of the Company. By 1836, the Company was incorporated

The library was the heart and soul of each literary society and provided the literature and reading materials to push an agenda for cultivating a generation of literate beings who were able to read the word and the world.

and had a library containing "nearly six hundred volumes of valuable historical, scientific, and miscellaneous works." This included encyclopedias, which were "a source of great mental profit to the members of the Company."

More than 20 years later, in 1854, the Banneker Literary Institute was established and maintained the same centrality of the library (Martin, 2002). A comprehensive library shelved with worldly texts served as the means to this end, and members set up a committee to catalogue the texts. The librarian's annual statement reported 482 volumes, comprising books and pamphlets purchased from The Smithsonian Institution and titles such as *Life of Captain John Brown, Life of Benjamin Banneker,* and *Register of Trades of Colored People.* These were examples of "useful books" articulated by Whipper in his earlier 1828 public address: "Members were required to donate a book to the group twice a month," and each donation was to be accompanied by a short speech, or a fine of 25 cents was issued. This provides record of the relationship of reading with oral language.

Using African American Newspapers as Texts

African American newspapers also played a vital role in textual reading, including *Freedom's Journal, The Colored American, The Genius of Universal Emancipation,* and *The Weekly Anglo-African.* Members of literary societies read and used newspaper issues as platforms to publish and share their writings publicly. They kept the community abreast of current events, announcements, and noteworthy information. The newspapers encouraged literary pursuits such as reading, writing, and practicing rhetorical skills (Bacon, 2007; Bacon & McClish, 2000; McHenry, 2002). These materials were easily accessible and informative, compelling, and responsive to the sociopolitical events and issues of the time. The periodical content offered a range of genres that served as educational tools and were in many ways the primary reading materials for literary societies. Some of the vignettes were short and convenient to read, while some were in the form of longer stories or narratives that may have promoted oral comprehension or were intended to be read aloud. Much like the social learning space of literary societies, examples of Black newspapers were consumable by a community of different reading abilities or "levels" and for readers of various ages (McHenry, 2002).

Informational pieces included articles, sermons, and reprinted public addresses set out to send messages to improve the moral and civic character of its readers. Other informational texts included announcements of marriages, deaths, "Domestic News," "Foreign News," minutes from various benevolent societies, and information on educating the population. Topics within these sections were equally diverse and presented a wide scope of news and information extended from their local context. Other articles pertained to current issues and the lives of emerging writers of the time. During the second week of circulation of *Freedom's Journal*, a biography of Phillis Wheatley was published. The article explained how her writings reflected the title and character of the journal, while also sharing with readers how she acquired and practiced literacy.

A reoccurring literary column of this same periodical featured a section of poems and broadsides by poets such as William Cullen Bryant and Phillis Wheatley. African Americans and others used their pens to speak truth into existence and to locate and project their voices. In the first issue, William Cullen Bryant penned a poem entitled "The African Chief," which told a story about a man once revered as a brave African warrior with beautiful adornments, who was now shackled and chained, taken to be a slave by men. In a later issue, two poems by Phillis Wheatley, "Hymn to Humanity" and "Hymn to the Morning," were published. Although poems like these spoke about the unrest and hope of the time, other poems such as "Forget Me Not" by F. G. Halleck exemplified love and passion. The poem "On the Poetic Muse," written by George Moses

Horton, presented a vivid account of how one can be absorbed in gentle and fluid thoughts and use poetry as a means for expression of such feelings:

> Far, far above this world I soar,
> And almost nature lose,
> Aerial regions to explore,
> With this ambitious Muse.
>
> My towering thoughts with pinions rise,
> Upon the gales of song,
> Which waft me through the mental skies,
> With music on my tongue.
>
> My Muse is all on mystic fire,
> Which kindles in my breast;
> To scenes remote she doth aspire,
> As never yet exprest.
>
> Wrapt in the dust she scorns to lie,
> Call'd by new charms away;
> Nor will she e'er refuse to try
> Such wonders to survey.
>
> Such is the quiet bliss of soul,
> When in some calm retreat,
> Where pensive thoughts like streamlets roll,
> And render silence sweet;
>
> And when the vain tumultuous crowd
> Shakes comfort from my mind,
> My muse ascends above the cloud
> And leaves the noise behind.
>
> With vivid flight she mounts on high
> Above the dusky maze,
> And with a perspicacious eye
> Doth far 'bove nature gaze.

The textual contributions of *Freedom's Journal* and other newspapers extended the pursuits of literary societies by offering them opportunities to expand their knowledge while providing them a vehicle to share their writings with the public. The journals, like the societies themselves, did not provide a singular profile of Black people. Instead, the texts nurtured various identities while at the same time assisting readers to engage in literary pursuits.

Selecting Texts for Classrooms and Schools Today

When selecting texts for the classroom, teachers need to consider the curriculum (what we teach) and the instruction (how we teach). The theories that frame teaching will impact both the curriculum and instruction. But the texts will enable the teaching of the curriculum. Teachers who rely exclusively on a textbook have already fallen short in their curriculum and instruction. Textbooks are not typically written to help with expanded goals for learning. We have to ask what texts can help our students accomplish. Texts should drive cognitive goals (skills and intellect) as well as critical analysis (criticality) and sociocultural goals (identity). As teachers consider texts for classroom use, I recommend that they ask themselves these questions:

1. What is worthwhile for learning in my content area?

2. Why did I choose this text to teach with? (This reason should go beyond the text being in the mandated curriculum.)

3. How have my students contributed to the selection of texts for teaching and learning?

4. When the curriculum/text provided by the school is not enough, how will I respond as a critical and equitable educator?

5. How will this text advance my students' learning of identity of themselves or other people/cultures?

6. How will this text advance my students' learning of skills?

7. How will this text advance my students' intellects? Is the text thought provoking?

8. How will this text advance my students' criticality? How does the text respond to the social times of the society?

9. How do my selected texts agitate the oppressors in the world?

10. What multimodal texts am I teaching with? (image, sound, video, performance, etc.)

11. Is the content and language of the book culturally authentic?

12. What are the backgrounds of the writer and illustrator of the text? Is there a stronger author I could use to bring students closer to the content?

13. How are students reading across genres and different literature in social studies, math, and science?

14. Where do I find engaging and enabling texts?

15. How will I determine whether my students were engaged in the text I selected?

Students must see themselves in the texts, including their cultures, identities, interests, experiences, desires, and future selves. Texts should teach multiple ideologies and perspectives. Teachers can find texts in public libraries, book lists online, and anthologies. Examples of selected texts may include cultural and African American anthologies, picture books, primary source documents, historic newspapers, poetry, laws, TED Talks, short stories, current news articles, art, photographs and pictures from visiting different cultural sites, and resistance writings penned by leading thinkers and activists.

Students must see themselves in the texts, including their cultures, identities, interests, experiences, desires, and future selves.

Using Text to Cultivate the Genius in Students and Teachers

When teaching the HRL Framework, here are some suggested approaches related to selecting and using texts.

Layering Texts

Educators "layer texts" when they teach and learn from multiple powerful and multimodal texts. These texts are print and nonprint and are intellectually compelling. Such texts can support the mandated curriculum, basal reader, or textbook. Much like we layer clothing to stay warm in cold temperatures and layer scents like perfumes, lotions, scrubs, body sprays, and so forth to smell better, I argue that when teachers layer multiple short, powerful, multimodal texts as they teach the four layered goals, students have a better chance at academic and personal success. Layered texts should help students understand local, national, and global communities and incite social critique, and should support the HRL Framework.

I argue that when teachers layer multiple short, powerful, multimodal texts as they teach the four layered goals, then students have a better chance at academic and personal success.

Textual Lineages

Alfred Tatum (2009) gave educators a gift when he published his research regarding textual lineages. Textual lineages are texts that are meaningful and significant in our lives. These books become part of our histories and lineages.

I like to think of textual lineages as my "family tree of books and other texts." We all remember certain movies, books, poetry, works of art, and other texts that have shaped our thinking and understanding of the world and ourselves. I think teachers should start with their own textual lineages of meaningful and significant literature and then look at their lists to see how much they have impacted their teaching of their content area. I find that teachers typically teach in ways that they were taught as children, even if that means teaching mostly European authors. They should also write out the professional texts (articles, reports, books, essays) that helped to shape their teaching and pedagogical approaches. Then teachers should have students write out their own textual lineages. I like to start with movies and then move to books, poems, and other texts. This becomes a diagnostic assessment to see which texts students have found meaningful in their lives and schooling. If their charts are blank, they shouldn't remain blank at the end of the school year. Their lineage chart also helps teachers to select the texts and types of texts that students are interested in.

Categories for Students and Teachers to Write Out Their Textual Lineages

- Movies/film
- TED Talks and other video
- Children's and young adult literature
- Digital texts
- Memes
- Social media posts
- Artwork

- Poetry
- Short stories
- Letters
- Historical artifacts
- Professional readings
- Blogs and websites

Teaching with Primary Source Documents

Primary source documents can help to historicize and intellectualize a wide variety of teaching topics by providing social and political thought across eras. These documents give accurate accounts of the perspectives of people who lived during that time. There is a history to every topic or concept, and teaching with these artifacts gives students more to investigate and think across. Also, these documents can provide a wider (and more truthful) history of people of color than textbooks provide.

Author and Context Textual Study

When teaching culturally and historically responsive texts, it is key to teach about the author and the context in which the text was written. This will help with the textual meaning and comprehension. Teaching in absence of this, one cannot fully teach the text.

- Who is the author?
- What is the author known for writing or writing about?
- Why did the writer write this text?
- What perspective has the author taken? Excluded?
- What was going on in the nation and world when this text was written?
- How does the social context alter or contribute to the meaning of the text?

HRL Curriculum Assessment Review

Teachers and administrators have to ask how much they question, review, assess, and evaluate the texts and curricula they are given to teach. We don't typically ask who wrote the curriculum and why. We don't measure the curriculum against the unique needs of our students and community. We must ask if the texts and overall curriculum are connected to the students' lives and are relevant and responsive. When I engage in curriculum audits, I ask:

How does each phase, chapter, or section in this curriculum (texts, passages, supporting documents, goals, assessment prompts, and guidance) explicitly address identities, skills, intellect, and criticality?

- **Identity:** How does the curriculum (including texts and exercises) help students to learn something about themselves and/or about others?

- **Skills:** How does the curriculum (including texts and exercises) respond to or build students' skills and standards?

- **Intellect:** How does the curriculum (including texts and exercises) respond to or build upon students' knowledge and mental powers? What are they becoming smarter about?

- **Criticality:** How does the curriculum (including texts and exercises) engage students' thinking about power and equity and the disruption of oppression?

Children's and young adult literature, like most packaged curricula and textbooks, lack diversity of authorship. Also, many curricula are written to focus on skills alone. Authors often feel it is easier to assess skills and not other pursuits of learning. This then becomes a capitalistic ploy, to gain financial wealth. In other words, there are people who profit from the failure of Black and Brown kids. If they only market programs around skills or around state learning standards (which were not written for all students), then they are easy to sell, because businesses and schools haven't traditionally valued identity development, intellect, or criticality over time. Publishers test and provide curricula on those goals they value most—those goals that marginalize certain groups. But if we want to move toward excellence, we have to assess and evaluate texts and curricula used in schools so we know with confidence the strengths and weaknesses of the curricula. We can then stop using inappropriate curricula and give students what they deserve.

Culturally and Historically Responsive Text

As a professor, I often have my teacher candidates engage in what I call, "Defend the Text." This is an exercise I created so that as they prepare to go into classrooms, they are extremely intentional about the text they choose to support their instruction—so they must defend every text selection. As they are doing so, they must express how the text has the

potential to advance the four layers of the HRL Framework. While historically textual reading was wide and varied and responded to multiple theoretical goals of learning, in schools and classrooms today, most texts are selected and taught to address skills at each student's level. This is why we see an overreliance on leveled texts, and consequently, students are labeled by their so-called reading levels—for example, "David is a 'Level G' reader"—or identified by their Lexile measure. Schools are notorious for looking at students' assessment scores from one test (that typically asks biased questions) and labeling students based on this one score. This reliance on test scores or reading "ability" is increasingly problematic because teachers begin to rely on this "skill identity" and neglect their students' other identities. Texts read during these assessments, such as guided reading books, may be watered down and lack cultural and historical responsiveness. To combat this, students

The Brownies' Book
JANUARY, 1920

One Dollar and a Half a Year   Fifteen Cents a Copy

need texts that restore their humanity and the true and diverse histories of the world. They need texts that teach them about themselves and equip them to face harsh realities of the world. Texts should incite new language, learning, and ways of thinking of the content. Connecting texts to the HRL Framework helps to have wider purposes for reading rather than just having goals of cognition. Culturally and historically responsive text selection has the potential to respond to students' identities, skills, intellect, and criticality.

Texts should incite new language, learning, and ways of thinking of the content.

Using Black history as a model for text selection and teaching helps teachers to be excellent in their profession and not basic. During and after the organization of literary societies, African Americans continued to advocate for representation of texts and cultivate their literacy and learning. Following the dissolution of literary societies, we see the emergence of the Brownie Stories in the early 1900s.

The Brownies' Book was published for children and their families. The literature held in this magazine was diverse and often featured many different genres. The readings were intended to be read with others in the family. Leading this effort was W. E. B. Du Bois, who stated that the texts were "designed for all children, but especially for ours." The texts represented people of color in a positive light, dispelling falsehood and stereotypes. I argue that the content of the readings was intended to recognize and cultivate the genius within youth. I often use this book to teach learning goals and to introduce youth to different genres, such as plays, folktales, and short stories. *The Brownies' Book* had seven goals, which included:

- To make colored children realize that being "colored" is a normal, beautiful thing.
- To make them familiar with the history and achievements of the Negro race.
- To help them understand that other colored children have grown into beautiful, useful, and famous persons.
- To teach them a delicate code of honor and action in their relations with White children.

- To turn their little hurts and resentments into emulation, ambition, and love of their homes and companions.

- To point out the best amusements and joys and worth-while things of life.

- To inspire them to prepare for definite occupations and duties with a broad spirit of sacrifice.

—W. E. B. Du Bois, "The True Brownies," *The Crisis*, October 1919

Even though literacy development was an organic goal, this list does not include goals such as passing a state assessment or reaching a particular "reading level" in guided reading. So why are those central goals in schools today? Returning to Black literary and literacy history means restoring excellence that is not just excellent for children of color, but for all children. This requires us to consider the purpose of the texts and literature we chose to support our instruction, as well as *the very purpose of schools.* I argue that schools and texts should help students to know themselves, their beauty, brilliance, and genius. They should also know the truth and histories of other groups of people who don't look like them. Schools and texts should help students learn the skills key to the content while also cultivating their intellect and building their knowledge and new ideas in the world. Finally, schools and texts should cultivate and nurture criticality so that young people won't read something and immediately take it as truth. Criticality while reading allows them to question knowledge so they are active learners.

Lesson Sample

Identity: Students will think of Haitian family culture and consider their own family when there is adversity. (*familial identity*)

Skills:

- **English/Language Arts:** Students will describe the relationship between a series of historical events, scientific ideas or concepts, or steps in technical procedures in a text, using language that pertains to time, sequence, and cause/effect.
- **Mathematics:** Students will learn about measuring the strength or magnitude of an earthquake and understand a Richter scale and seismograph.
- **Science:** Students will study earthquakes and natural disasters.
- **Social Studies:** Students will learn about the history of Haiti and Haitian people.

Intellect: Students will learn about the country of Haiti and the earthquake that struck in 2010.

Criticality: Students will learn about the concept of resiliency and how it relates to the history and people of Haiti.

Layered Texts:

- *Eight Days: A Story of Haiti* by Edwidge Danticat
- Audio interview with author Edwidge Danticat
- Informational text/article and a video on earthquakes
- Map of Haiti
- Images of earthquakes, Haiti, and Haitian culture
- Primary source documents related to Haiti and Haitian culture

Teachers must think of texts as the core and center of their teaching. The texts teachers select for students could make or break a lesson plan. So it is key to continually reflect on the purpose each text serves toward the goals of the HRL Framework. Further, if texts are the vehicles or means for excellent teaching and learning, then teachers need rich literature to select from, and it would be helpful if texts were provided at the school.

Questions for Further Consideration: Teachers and Preservice Teachers

1. What types of literature, books, or texts are present in your classroom libraries? What types of texts and authors are missing? Is the literature representative of the lives and times of the students in the building?
2. How do you select literature to teach your lesson or unit plans?
3. How do you involve students in text selection of the classroom library and for lesson/unit plans?
4. How could layered multimodal text enrich your teaching and learning?
5. What professional texts are you reading to help your learning and teaching of identity development, skills, intellect, and criticality?

Questions for Further Consideration: Principals and School Leaders

1. What types of literature, books, or texts are present in your school library or media center? What types of texts and authors are missing? Is the literature representative of the lives and times of the students in the building?
2. What frequent culturally and historically responsive assessment do you arrange for the critical review of mandated curriculum? Do you just expect teachers to teach what they are told to teach, or do you question and review it for yourself? Are students involved in this review?
3. How do you use funds for culturally and historically responsive books each year?
4. Do you have professional development to help teachers with ways to teach these culturally and historically responsive books?
5. How do you involve students in text selection for the school library or media center?
6. What types of scholarship and research books do you engage teachers for book studies? How are these book clubs organized? How are professional learning texts selected?

CHAPTER 8

Using Historically Responsive Lesson Plans

We wish to plead our own cause. Too long have others spoken for us. Too long has the public been deceived by misrepresentations, in things which concern us dearly...

Education being an object of the highest importance to the welfare of society, we shall endeavour to present just and adequate views of it, and to urge upon our brethren the necessity and expediency of training their children, while young, to habits of industry, and thus forming them for becoming useful members of society. It is surely time that we should awake from this lethargy of years, and make a concentrated effort for the education of our youth.

—*Freedom's Journal*, **March 16, 1827**

This was printed in the inaugural issue of *Freedom's Journal*, the first African American newspaper, in which Black people owned, edited, and operated. Printed on March 16, 1827, editors Samuel E. Cornish and John Russwurm wanted a platform for anti-racism and for community uplift as most of the Black men and women in the country were still enslaved and experiencing acts of terrorism on their lives. This newsprint was also a mechanism to reclaim the authority and power of language, as language had been used to create false and deficit narratives about Black lives. In many ways, the opening line, "We wish to plead our own cause," signaled a public declaration to express their mission of efforts in literacy and literacy development. Pleading their own cause meant they wanted to set and build their own agenda for progress. And this progress centered on education, especially for the youth who would become the next generations of leading readers, writers, and thinkers. These words sparked the movement for literary societies and other literacy pursuits, as well as intellectual activism (Martin, 2002). This included David Walker's *Appeal*, the development of African-centered schools, and the organization of literary societies.

This proclamation has also served well in my own pursuit to advance the state of education and to reorient education today toward the historical literary excellence of Blackness. In this book, I described the educational pursuits of Black people in and around literary societies of the 19th century and discussed a four-layered equity framework for providing a full and comprehensive education for all youth with the goal of teaching the whole child across all disciplinary areas. The four layers of the Historically Responsive Literacy Framework allow us to plead our own cause today, while making education the highest objective for our young people. This model, although informed by Black history, is productive for all. It adheres to multiple theoretical lenses of education while attending to students' personal and academic achievement.

The Historically Responsive Literacy Framework

The HRL Framework advances the Common Core State Standards by moving beyond just skills and knowledge. This calls for a shifting of schools' curriculum and lesson planning to be inclusive of Black history, as we prepare preservice teachers and support practicing teachers. When these four learning goals are taught using excellent methods of teaching, learning becomes humanizing. I suggest some methods and approaches throughout the chapters. If we are to be responsive to the cultural and racial identities of our students and our times, we must recast any learning standard frameworks that are skills-oriented to be more inclusive of identity, intellect, and criticality so that these new frameworks, derived from history, become the pathway to improving education for all students, and also become a gauge to measure the quality of learning and teaching. Collectively, these four pursuits are also intended to restore the power, energy, and originality of teachers and leaders.

To teach historically responsive literacy and still meet the requirements of the district curriculum standards, I offer a lesson plan template below along with sample lessons/units from practicing teachers.

HRL Lesson Plan Template

Name of Lesson:	Grade Level:

Teacher:

Length of Lesson: *Briefly write the anticipated length of the planned lesson in days and indicate the number of minutes per class session.*

Students' Identities and Background: *Write a brief description of the students' identities—including their cultural identities. Who are the students who will be taught in this class?*

Learning Goals	Include the four HRL learning goals. These goals must be clear. They are also measurable/assessable and should be linked to students' cultures/identities, personal and academic needs, and district learning standards. Objectives for excellent lesson plans should be written to advance students' identity development, skills/proficiencies, intellectual development, and criticality. You may begin statements with "Students will.../Students will be able to," or use direct/action verbs to state what students will do during the teaching and learning. **Identities:** How will your teaching help students to learn something about themselves and/or others? **Skills:** What skills and content learning standards are you teaching? **Intellect:** What will your students become smarter about? **Criticality:** How will you engage your thinking about power, equity, and anti-oppression in the text, in society and in the world?
Layered Texts	List (include authors) the selected texts you have chosen to support student learning (including print and non-print sources; links). Attach copies of all supporting, layered text.
Vocabulary & Concepts	Include the central vocabulary words and concepts from the central reading.
Student Spark	State how the teacher will get students excited and engaged in the learning to come. This is an opportunity to include multimodal text and critical questions. This should only be about 5–7 minutes.
Body of Lesson	Write out an overview of the entire lesson plan.
Closure	State what the teacher will do to close the lesson.
Assessment	For each learning goal, write out how each will be assessed.

TM ® & © Scholastic Inc. All rights reserved. From *Cultivating Genius* copyright © 2020 by Gholdy Muhammad. Published by Scholastic Inc.

Sample Lesson and Unit Plans

Below are six sample lessons and unit plans across grade levels and content areas to demonstrate the flexibility and applicability of the HRL Framework.

2nd Grade Literacy

Teacher: Daray Simmons

HRL Learning Goals: Change Makers

Identity: Students will consider their community identities and decide upon an issue in their community that needs attention.

Skill: Students will be able to write a persuasive essay.

Intellect: Students will learn what it means to be a change maker.

Criticality: Students will come up with an action plan to solve the identified problems in their communities.

Layered Texts:

- *Change Makers* by Libby Martinez
- article, "How Did Martin Luther King's Vision Change the World?"
- Kelvin Doe at TEDxTeen

3rd–5th Grade Computer Science

Teacher: Patricia Wong

HRL Learning Goals: A Name Is Just a Name, Right?

Identity: Students will become more self-aware of their own identities and learn ways to respect other individualities.

Skill: Students will use the computer as a tool for generating ideas using computerized devices and systems through coding and programming.

Intellect: Students will learn the concepts of identity, diversity, and inclusion.

Criticality: Students will understand how diversity affects the world and how inclusion can build a better world for all.

Layered Texts:

- YouTube video on names (https://www.youtube.com/watch?v=0EP80JcIJuU)
- *My Name Is Sangoel* by Karen Lynn Williams and Khadra Mohammed
- short biographies of Michelle Obama, Sonia Maria Sotomayor, and Post Malone
- TED Talk on facial recognition software by Joy Buolamwini

6th Grade English Language Arts

Teacher: Leo Singleton

HRL Learning Goals: Writing the Fantasy Genre

Identity: Students will think about the identities of people of color and their experiences with the genre of fantasy.

Skill: Students will learn about setting and describe fantasy settings.

Intellect: Students will learn about potential setting locations outside of Europe and the history of fantasy writers who are not European and their setting choices.

Criticality: Students will consider the negative impact of the privileging of certain settings in the genre of fantasy on people of color.

Layered Texts:

- *Black Panther* movie clip
- multiple images of fantasy film scenes
- map of the world
- images of Wonders of the World
- book covers of fantasy fiction written by authors of color
- short excerpts of fantasy fiction
- student writing

8th Grade English Language Arts

Teacher: Perez Beltethon

HRL Learning Goals: Colorism—"God Help the Child"

Identity: Students will think about their physical appearance, specifically their skin tone, and discuss how they navigate society through perception of their skin tone.

Skill: Students will read and comprehend images, clips, and an excerpt from "God Help the Child" by Toni Morrison, and write a journal entry to demonstrate comprehension.

Intellect: Students will learn about the concept of colorism.

Criticality: Students will learn about structures set up to oppress people based on skin color, even within their own race and ethnicity.

Layered Texts:

- *God Help the Child* excerpt by Toni Morrison
- Meme that is based on colorism, a clip from *Black-ish* (https://www.youtube.com/watch?v=fB812yqDwPM)

9th Grade Dance Survey

Teacher: DeAngelo Blanchard

HRL Learning Goals: Artistic Perspective

Identity: Students will connect with their artistic insight and ability.

Skill: Students will analyze and interpret artistic work.

Intellect: Students will connect their understanding of dance with opera and Leontyne Price.

Criticality: Students will find agency in their skills to critically analyze art.

10th–12th Grade World Literature

Teacher: Evan Braunschweiger

HRL Learning Goals: Telling Our Stories

Identity: Students will think about themselves as writers and consider the stories in their lives that were most influential shaping their sense of self.

Skill: Students will learn narrative writing techniques.

Intellect: Students will learn more about life and times of the person written about in their selected narratives.

Criticality: Students will learn about the powers and barriers that impede success, academic or otherwise, in communities of color.

Layered Texts:

- "Learning to Read" (excerpt from *Autobiography of Malcolm X*, as told to Alex Haley)
- excerpts from *The Freedom Writers' Diary* by Erin Gruwell and the Freedom Writers
- "Mixtapes Saved My Career" (excerpt from *The Autobiography of Gucci Mane* by Gucci Mane with Neil Martinez-Belkin)
- "The House on Mango Street" and "My Name" (vignettes from *The House on Mango Street* by Sandra Cisneros)
- "How to be Black" (excerpt from *How to Be Black* by Baratunde Thurston)
- "Little Things Are Big" (short story by Jesús Colón)
- Selected film clips from *Freedom Writers* (2007)

11th Grade English

Teacher: Keeyah Hicks

HRL Learning Goals: Character Development in "I Know Why the Caged Bird Sings"

Identity: Students will explain the interconnected role race and power play in society.

Skill: Students will learn how complex characters develop over the course of a text and write a response to examine and convey their ideas clearly and accurately.

Intellect: Students will learn about the concept of adversity.

Criticality: Students will analyze and justify the character's (Momma) actions when faced with a racially tense/life threatening encounter.

Layered Texts:

- music video of Tupac's "Brenda's Got a Baby"
- *I Know Why the Caged Bird Sings* by Maya Angelou
- video clip from movie *I Know Why the Caged Bird Sings*
- various images related to the book and videos
- plot diagrams

These lessons and units are a part of a growing list of examples and samples that teachers and preservice teachers have developed with me over the past several years. The teachers work across content areas, and we have to consider what these lessons or units would look like if we removed goals of identity, intellect, and criticality. Here is another example of a physical education unit plan on the teaching of lacrosse. The teacher, who taught at a school for boys, wanted to introduce his students to lacrosse, but they only wanted to play basketball. Naturally, my next response was, "Teach them lacrosse." To help the teacher, I created the following lesson plan.

Oftentimes, P.E. teachers may feel left out, so it was important for him to know that he, too, could teach in culturally and historically responsive ways.

Identity: Students will learn the physical (bodily) benefits of engaging in lacrosse. (*physical identity*)

Skill: Students will learn how to play lacrosse.

Intellect: Students will learn the history of lacrosse within and outside of indigenous groups and communities of color.

Criticality: Students will unpack race and sports. What are the politics of lacrosse (accessibility)?

The identity goal allows youth to learn what happens to their body when they are actively engaged in a sport like lacrosse and which muscles are used and exercised. The skill for P.E. is learning how to play lacrosse. The intellect goal is learning about the history of lacrosse, especially its history among indigenous people.

Sports also enables us to examine the history of race and criticality as it relates to sports, whether athletes are putting a Black power fist in the air or kneeling during "The Star-Spangled Banner." This is why the criticality goal is written to talk about race and sports and the accessibility of the sport. Although it has a history with Native peoples, it is widely more accessible in wealthy schools with mostly White students.

The texts create a space for youth to read, write, and think in physical education and maintain the same literacies that they experience and should experience in other classes.

Layered texts include an article on Jim Brown. Brown is mostly known for his football career but not as much for his time playing lacrosse. Brown told *The New York Times* in 1984 that "Lacrosse is probably the best sport I have ever played." Other texts to layer would include images of lacrosse across different groups of people, articles around athlete protest, a video on the history of lacrosse, and photographs of the lacrosse stick across time. The texts would create a space for youth to read, write, and think in physical education and maintain the same literacies that they experience and should experience in other classes.

Moving Toward Historical Excellence

As I conclude, I want to implicitly add one more "layer" that helped to structure the literacy development of early readers and writers. This is love. Love was absorbed in all of their pursuits of literacy development. They loved to work toward the four pursuits and received great fulfillment from engaging with meaningful and significant texts. bell hooks said that, "A generous heart is always open, always ready to receive our going and coming. In the midst of such love we need never fear abandonment. This is the most precious gift true love offers—the experience of knowing we always belong" (hooks, 2001). We have an absence of love across many schools. Teachers and leaders must love the ways our children talk, learn, smile, look, sound, the ways they are loud, and the ways they are silent. Before we get to the curriculum and standards, our students need to know they are loved. bell hooks said that love is always knowing that we belong. But we don't just need love but a critical love that works to disrupt and dismantle oppression. Martin Luther King Jr. once said that love and power must be in a harmonious balance:

> *But we don't just need love but a critical love that works to disrupt and dismantle oppression.*

> One of the great problems of history is that the concepts of love and power have usually been contrasted as opposites— polar opposites—so that love is identified with a resignation of power, and power with a denial of love ... What is needed is the realization that power without love is reckless and abusive, and that love without power is sentimental and anemic. Power at its best is love implementing the demands of justice, and justice at its best is love correcting everything that stands against love.

What I appreciate about his words is that he connects two things that are typically polar opposites of each other—love and power. But when we look at education, both play an extremely important role. We have power as teachers and school leaders. We have to be prudent with our power because power without love is harmful, it is detrimental—indeed, it is reckless. Critical love is leading schools toward anti-oppression. It goes beyond acts of care, but it is authentically about embodying a great deal of concern, compassion, and empathy. And it is an action, not just a feeling, that pushes toward making sure no one experiences marginalization of any kind. It is a choice in our leadership practices. I want us all to make this choice and make critical love the center of what we do for children. Critical love will serve as the foundation for what we do moving forward with teaching and learning.

In another archive from *The Weekly Advocate*, the author explained the purpose of reading and implicitly captures the sentiments of critical love:

> By reading, you may visit all countries, converse with the wise, good, and great, who have lived in any age or country, imbibe their very feelings and sentiments and view every thing elegant in architecture, sculpture, and painting. By reading you may ascend to those remote regions where other spheres encircle other suns, where other stars illuminate a new expanse of skills and enkindle the most sublime emotions that can animate the human soul.

During the mid-19th century, if you were a person of color, particularly an African American, your life was surrounded by racism, sexism, and other oppressions.

Literacy and acts of reading were linked to liberation and freedom. If you were caught reading, you were arrested, physically punished, or worse, killed. In the North, Black people held some liberties and freedoms, yet were still oppressed. In the freedoms they held, they gravitated to books for identity, skill, intellect, and criticality, but also to develop their artistic sensibilities. Though many couldn't physically travel abroad, they journeyed via literature to explore foreign lands. Reading created the space and opportunity to converse with the wise and the intellectuals of the world. People of color conversed with authors who lived across ages and eras—and through reading, they were able to experience the beauty offered in the word and the world. The writer goes on to state that by reading, you can be in full observance of elegance. By reading you can ascend. I quickly noticed that the language of ascent means something quite different than merely *traveling*. To ascend means to climb or to gain upward mobility. It means to lead and to rise. They sought to ascend to the far and distant areas of the world— spheres of knowledge that are distinguished and refined. By reading, the writer asserts, one can enkindle the most beautiful, emotions that are so fulfilling—so nourishing that it can animate your human soul. Isn't that beautiful?

It is this beauty and purpose of reading and of literacy that should frame education in schools today. This is how we want our students in our schools to experience literacy. We should want to move beyond mere grades and test scores and make it our mission that when students leave our teachers and our schools, they not only earn strong grades and test scores, but they *also* embody a love and joy for reading and literacy—that they leave us and ascend to remote regions of the world while also discovering the power of their own minds. This is the genius that they are craving for others to cultivate—to prepare, to raise, to grow, and to help develop. Cultivating genius speaks to the responsibility and work that educators have. We must keep ourselves accountable to this responsibility, because it's for our students and their families, not to a state test. If we want different results as a nation and as a world, we must do something different. For so long, education in classrooms has remained largely the same. Historically Responsive Literacy is a dynamic change for our students of color to provide them the education to which they are entitled. This change will result in the elevation and transformation of education.

I argue throughout this book that we need more than small movement or change in education, but transformation. And transformation has to be collaborative. This level of change does not happen if our universities, schools (and leadership), and communities are not working toward this progress. Like the African proverb says, *It takes a village.* A village is a supportive and trusting group of people who would want for you what they want for themselves; they are not jealous, nor do they envy your pursuit toward justice. Instead they strive to make you great(er) because your triumph is their triumph; when you have good news, their first reaction is to be happy for you and to celebrate your light. The question becomes, who is in your village? In other words, who will help you to strive toward teaching and learning in this way? It is key that your village is not just new teachers or those who struggle with pedagogy. Instead, there needs to be a balance of mentors and experts in teaching and learning. Your village must consist of educators, communities, and partners who are committed to the goals of equity, social justice, and transformation—educators who are ready to move toward action. Because when we return to the excellence in literacy education and move toward history in ways described in this book, we find that it gives our students a chance to lead fulfilled and quality lives while also giving them the agency to transform the world around them and build a better humanity for all.

History for the Future:
An Afterword by Maisha T. Winn

*H*istory Matters. This is the first of four pedagogical stances I introduced that are essential for paradigm shifting toward justice in schools (Winn, 2018). The three additional stances—*Race Matters*, *Justice Matters*, and *Language Matters*—are represented by nested circles, with *History Matters* making up the outermost circle. This reminds educators that our own histories, as well as those belonging to our students, school communities, and surrounding neighborhoods, must be given consideration if stakeholders in schools are to engage in productive relationships. We need to ensure that academic literacy and instruction for students from nondominant communities are not replaced with forms of literacy that privilege and are contingent upon students' sociohistorical lives, both proximally and distally (Gutierrez, 2008). Enter Gholdy Muhammad and her courageous and beautiful book that leverages historically responsive literacies to cultivate the genius that is in our children and youth that all too often goes untapped. Beginning with early Black Americans' quest for literacy—in spite of it being illegal and punishable by physical harm and death—and moving into early African American literary societies, Muhammad provides the context for this genius that is often overlooked and underutilized. While scholars have examined Black literate lives (Fisher, 2009) and the levers used to pursue literacy in spite of systematic attempts to undermine these efforts, to date no one has demonstrated how to put these histories to work for younger generations of writers, readers, and thinkers.

I situate Muhammad's text at the intersection of *History Matters* and a newer stance, *Futures Matter* (Winn, 2019), in that she provides pedagogical portraits of leveraging history to support young people in imagining their futures as writers, readers, thinkers, and "doers" of the world. Muhammad's four-layered framework pursuing Identity,

Skills, Intellect, and Criticality is precisely what educators need to bolster their teaching efforts in a sociopolitical climate that can be polarizing and isolating. This framework provides purpose in the work to those of us who consider ourselves to be allies of children and youth and—most importantly—a clear roadmap to do the work. So many books leave us wondering, waiting, and wishing. However, Muhammad fills all the voids in the work, demonstrating how history, historiography, and historicizing our young people and their families will create and sustain futures.

Fisher, M. T. (2009). *Black literate lives: Historical and contemporary perspectives.* New York: Routledge.

Gutierrez, K. D. (2008). Language and literacies as civil rights. In S. Greene's (Editor). *Literacy as a civil right: Reclaiming social justice in literacy teaching and learning* (169–184). New York: Peter Lang.

Winn, M. T. (2018). *Justice on both sides: Transforming education through restorative justice.* Cambridge: Harvard Education Press.

Winn, M. T. (2019). *Paradigm shifting toward justice.* University of Michigan, TeachingWorks. http://www.teachingworks.org/images/files/Winn_TeachingWorks.pdf

Maisha T. Winn is the Chancellor's Leadership Professor in the School of Education at the University of California, Davis, and codirector of the Transformative Justice in Education Center. She is the author of multiple titles including *Humanizing Research: Decolonizing Qualitative Inquiry with Youth and Communities* coauthored with Django Paris and *Writing Instruction in the Culturally Relevant Classroom* coauthored with Latrise P. Johnson.

References

Adichie, C. N., Films for the Humanities & Sciences (Firm), & Films Media Group. (2009). *TEDTalks: Chimamanda Adichie—The danger of a single story*. New York: Films Media Group.

Alvermann, D. E., Ruddell, R. B., & Unrau, N. J. (Eds.) (2013). *Theoretical models and processes of reading* (6th ed.). Newark, DE: International Reading Association.

Anderson, J. D. (1988). *The education of Blacks in the South, 1860–1935*. Chapel Hill: University of North Carolina Press.

Bacon, J. (2007). *Freedom's journal: The first African-American newspaper*. Lanham, MD: Lexington Books.

Bacon, J., & McClish, G. (2000). Reinventing the master's tools: Nineteenth-century African-American literary societies of Philadelphia and rhetorical education. *Rhetoric Society Quarterly, 30*(4), 19–47.

Beck, A. (2005). A place for critical literacy. *Journal of Adolescent and Adult Literacy, 48*(5), 392–400.

Bell, H. H. (1958). The American Moral Reform Society, 1836–1841. *The Journal of Negro Education, 27*(1), 34.

Belt-Beyan, P. M. (2004). *The emergence of African American literacy traditions: Family and community efforts in the nineteenth century*. Westport, CT: Praeger Publishers.

Brettell, C. (2000). Fieldwork in the archives: Methods and sources of historical anthropology. In H. R. Bernard (Ed.), *Handbook of methods in cultural anthropology* (pp. 513–546). Lanham, MD: Altamira Press.

Brown, R. N. (2013). *Hear our truths: The creative potential of Black girlhood*. Urbana, Chicago, IL: University of Illinois Press.

Cornelius, J. (1983). "We slipped and learned to read": Slave accounts of the literacy process, 1830-1865. *Phylon, 44*(3), 171–186.

Delpit, L. D. (2006). *Other people's children: Cultural conflict in the classroom*. New York: New Press.

Diamondstone, J. (2002). Language education in English education: Grammar instruction, grammar plus, or critical social analysis? *Teaching Education, 13*(3), 317–328.

Douglass, F., & American Abolition Society. (1857). *Two speeches, by Frederick Douglass: One on West India emancipation, delivered at Canandaigua, Aug. 4th: and the other on the Dred Scott decision, delivered in New York, on the occasion of the anniversary of the American Abolition Society, May, 1857*.

Facing History and Ourselves National Foundation. (2015). *The reconstruction era: The fragility of democracy*.

Fisher, M. T. (2004). "The song is unfinished": The new literate and literary and their institutions. *Written Communication, 21*(3), 290–312.

Fisher, M. T. (2009). *Black literate lives: Historical and contemporary perspectives*. New York: Routledge.

Freire, P., & Macedo, D. (1987). *Literacy: Reading the word and the world*. South Hadley, MA: Bergin & Garvey.

Gay, G. (2000). *Culturally responsive teaching: Theory, research, and practice*. New York: Teachers College Press.

Gay, G. (2002). Preparing for culturally responsive teaching. *Journal of Teacher Education, 53*(2), 106–116.

Gay, G. (2010). *Culturally responsive teaching: Theory, research, and practice, 2nd edition*. New York: Teachers College Press.

Gayles, G. W. (Ed.) (2003). *Conversations with Gwendolyn Brooks*. Jackson, MS: University Press of Mississippi.

Gee, J. P. (2000). Identity as an analytic lens for research in education. *Review of Research in Education, 25*(1), 99–125.

Ginwright, S., & James, T. (2002). From assets to agents of change: Social justice, organizing, and youth development. *New Directions for Student Leadership, 96*, 27–46.

Giroux, H. (1987). Literacy and the pedagogy of empowerment. In P. Freire & D. Macedo (Eds.), *Literacy: Reading the word and the world* (pp. 1–29). Portsmouth, NH: Heinemann.

Guinier, L. (2004). From racial liberalism to racial literacy: Brown v. Board of Education and the interest-divergence dilemma. *Journal of American History, 91*(1), 92–118.

Gutierrez, K. D. (2008). Developing a sociocritical literacy in the third space. *Reading Research Quarterly, 43*, 148–164.

Harris, V. J. (1992). African-American conceptions of literacy: A historical perspective. *Theory Into Practice, 31*(4), 276–286.

hooks, b. (2001). *All about love: New visions*. New York: Perennial.

Huyck, D., & Dahlen, S. P. (2019 June 19). Diversity in children's books 2018. sarahpark.com blog. Created in consultation with Edith Campbell, Molly Beth Griffin, K. T. Horning, Debbie Reese, Ebony Elizabeth Thomas, and Madeline Tyner, with statistics compiled by the Cooperative Children's Book Center, School of Education, University of Wisconsin-Madison:http://ccbc.education.wisc.edu/books/pcstats.asp. Retrieved from https://readingspark.wordpress.com/2019/06/19/picture-this-diversity-in-childrens-books-2018-infographic/

Jetton, T. L., & Shanahan, C. (2012). *Adolescent literacy in the academic disciplines: General principles and practical strategies*. New York: The Guilford Press.

Johnston, E., D'Andrea Montalbano, P., & Kirkland, D. E. (2017). *Culturally responsive education: A primer for policy and practice*. New York: Metropolitan Center for Research on Equity and the Transformation of Schools, New York University.

Kallus, M. K., & Ratliff, P. (2011). Reading: A brief history to 1899. In J. B. Cobb & M. K. Kallus (Eds.), *Historical, theoretical and sociological foundations of reading in the United States*. Boston: Pearson.

King, M. L., Jr., & Carson, C. (1998). *The autobiography of Martin Luther King, Jr*. Intellectual Properties Management.

Kohl, H. (1983). Examining closely what we do. *Learning, 12*(1), 28–30.

Kynard, C. (2010). From candy girls to cyber sista-cipher: Narrating Black females' color-consciousness and counterstories in and out of school. *Harvard Educational Review, 80*(1), 30–52.

Ladson-Billings, G. (1994). *The dreamkeepers: Successful teachers of African American children.* San Francisco: Jossey-Bass.

Ladson-Billings, G. (1995). Toward a theory of culturally relevant pedagogy. *American Educational Research Journal, 32*(3), 465–491.

Ladson-Billings, G. (2014). Culturally relevant pedagogy 2.0: a.k.a. the Remix. *Harvard Educational Review, 84*(1), 74–84.

Lee, C. D. (1995). A culturally based cognitive apprenticeship: Teaching African American high school students skills in literary interpretation. *Reading Research Quarterly, 30,* 608–630.

Love, B. L. (2019). *We want to do more than survive: Abolitionist teaching and the pursuit of educational freedom.* Boston: Beacon Press.

Luke, A. (2000). Critical literacy in Australia: A matter of context and standpoint. *Journal of Adolescent & Adult Literacy, 43*(5), 448–461.

Martin, T. (2002). The Banneker Literary Institute of Philadelphia: African American intellectual activism before the war of the slaveholders' rebellion. *The Journal of African American History, 87,* 303–322.

McHenry, E. (2002). *Forgotten readers: Recovering the lost history of African American literary societies.* Durham, NC: Duke University Press.

McHenry, E., & Heath, S. B. (1994). The literate and the literary: African Americans as writers and readers—1830-1940. *Written Communication, 11,* 419–443.

Moje, E. B., Luke, A., Davies, B., & Street, B. (2009). Literacy and identity: Examining the metaphors in history and contemporary research. *Reading Research Quarterly, 44*(4). 415–437.

Moll, L., & González, N. (1994). Lessons from research with language minority children. *Journal of Reading Behavior, 26*(4), 23–41.

Muhammad, G. E., & Haddix, M. (2016). Centering Black girls' ways of knowing: A historical review of literature on the multiple literacies of Black girls, *English Education, 48*(4), 299–336.

Muhammad, G, E. (2018). A plea for identity and criticality: Reframing literacy learning standards through a four-layered model. *Journal of Adolescent & Adult Literacy, 62*(2), 137–142.

Muhammad, G. E. (2019). Protest, power, and possibilities: The need for agitation literacies. *Journal of Adolescent & Adult Literacy.*

Mullings, L., & Marable, M. (2009). *Let nobody turn us around: An African American anthology* (Vol. 2nd ed). Lanham, MD: Rowman & Littlefield Publishers.

National Center for Education Statistics. (2018). *National assessment of educational progress: An overview of NAEP.* Washington, D.C.: National Center for Education Statistics, Institute of Education Sciences, U.S. Dept. of Education.

Newkirk, P. (Ed.) (2009). *Letters from Black America: Intimate portraits of the African American experience.* Boston: Beacon Press.

Noguera, P. A. (2003). The trouble with Black boys: The role and influence of environmental and cultural factors on the academic performance of African American males. *Urban Education, 38*(4), 431–59

Omi, M., & Winant, H. (1994). *Racial formation in the United States from the 1960s to the 1990s, 2nd ed.* New York: Routledge.

Paris, D. (2012). Culturally sustaining pedagogy: A needed change in stance, terminology, and practice. *Educational Researcher, 41*(3), 93–97.

Paris, D., & Alim, H. S. (2017). *Culturally sustaining pedagogies: Teaching and learning for justice in a changing world.* New York: Teacher's College Press.

Porter, D. (1936). The organized educational activities of Negro literary societies, 1828–1856. *Journal of Negro History, 5,* 555–576.

Porter, D. (1995). *Early Negro writing 1760–1837.* Baltimore, MD: Black Classic Press.

Ramsey, A. E., Sharer, W. B., L'Eplattenier, B., & Mastrangelo, L. S. (Eds.). (2010). *Working in the archives: Practical research methods for rhetoric and composition.* Carbondale, IL: Southern Illinois University Press.

Royster, J. J. (2000). *Traces of a stream: Literacy and social change among African American women.* Pittsburgh, PA: University of Pittsburgh Press.

Schiller, B. (2008). Learning their letters: Critical literacy, epistolary culture, and slavery in the antebellum south. *Southern Quarterly, 45*(3), 11–29.

Sealey-Ruiz, Y. (2013). Toward a pedagogy of racial literacy in first year composition. *Teaching English in a Two-Year College (TETYC), 40*(3), 384–398

Skerrett, A. (2011). English teachers' racial literacy knowledge and practice. *Race Ethnicity and Education, 14*(3), 313–330.

Sutherland, L. (2005). Black adolescent girls' use of literacy practices to negotiate boundaries of ascribed identity. *Journal of Literacy Research, 37*(3), 365–406, Fall 2005.

Tatum, A. W. (2006). Engaging African American males in reading. *Educational Leadership, 63*(5), 44–49.

Tatum, A. W. (2009). *Reading for their life: Rebuilding the textual lineages of African American adolescent males.* Portsmouth, NH: Heinemann.

Tatum, A. W., & Muhammad, G. E. (2012). African American males and literacy development in contexts that are characteristically urban. *Urban Education, 47*(2), 434–463.

Woodson, C. G. (2015). *Negro orators and their orations.* Start Publishing.

Zuidema, L. A. (2012). The grammar workshop: Systematic language study in reading and writing contexts. *English Journal, 101*(5), 63–71.

Zumwalt, K., & Craig, E. (2005). Teachers' characteristics: Research on the demographic profile. In M. Cochran-Smith & K. M. Zeichner (Eds.), *Studying teacher education: The report of the AERA panel on research and teacher education* (pp. 111–156). Mahwah, NJ: Erlbaum.

Index